HYDROPONICS
FOR
BEGINNERS

The Essential Guide For Absolute Beginners To Easily Build An Inexpensive DIY Hydroponic System At Home. Grow Vegetables, Fruit And Herbs With Hydroponic Gardening Secrets.

By
Richard Jones

© Copyright 2020 Richard Jones
All Rights Reserved

Legal Notice

The content within this book may not be amended, reproduced, duplicated, sold, used or transmitted without direct written permission from the author or the publisher.

Disclaimer Notice

The information provided in this book is for education purposes only. This book is designed to provide helpful information on the subjects discussed and motivation to our reader. All effort has been executed to present accurate, up to date, and reliable, complete information. No warranties of any kind are declared or implied. Readers acknowledge that the author is not engaging in the rendering of legal, financial, medical or professional advice. Please consult a licensed professional before attempting any techniques outlined in this book.

Under no circumstances will any blame or legal responsibility be held against the publisher, or author, for any damages, reparation, or monetary loss due either directly or indirectly to the information contained within this book, including, but not limited to, errors, omissions or inaccuracies.

Table Of Contents

TABLE OF CONTENTS	3
FOREWORD	5
INTRODUCTION	9
INTRODUCTION TO HYDROPONICS	15
ADVANTAGES AND DISADVANTAGES OF HYDROPONICS	33
TERMINOLOGY USED IN HYDROPONICS	40
HYDROPONIC GROWING SYSTEMS	51
EQUIPMENT & THINGS YOU'LL NEED	65
HOW TO ASSEMBLE A DIY HYDROPONIC SYSTEM STEP-BY-STEP	79
THE GROWING MEDIUM	91
STARTING SEEDS	101
THE BEST PLANTS TO CHOOSE FOR HYDROPONICS	121
NUTRIENT SOLUTIONS	129
PEST AND DISEASE CONTROL	142
HOW TO FIX THE MOST COMMON NUTRITION PROBLEMS	161
THE FIGHT AGAINST PLANT DISEASES	171
MYTHS AND MISTAKES TO AVOID	181
CONCLUSION	196

Foreword

Do you want to learn how to easily build an inexpensive DIY hydroponic growing system, cultivate organic vegetables, fruit and herbs at home with hydroponics? If yes, then keep reading...

Hydroponics is used as a controlled agriculture system for growing out of season crops, for producing crops in areas that are less suited for growing crops, and in areas where the water supply cannot support conventional farming. Research centers also take up hydroponics to grow crops they need to study plant nutrition, plant breeding, and plant diseases because the conditions under which the crops are grown can be regulated as desired. Almost all plants can be grown using hydroponics.

When crops are grown in this way, they use up 50% less land and 90% less water when contrasted with traditional crop growing methods. However, the yields from the crops are 4 times more, and the crop growth rate is twice as fast when using hydroponics. This is possible because the crops have everything they would need, at the right concentrations.

In place of the soil used in typical agriculture, the farmer or gardener roots the plants in compounds like vermiculite, clay pellets or rock wool. All substances used must be inert so that they do not introduce any new elements into the plant's environment. The solution of water and nutrients is then poured over the support material so that the plant can feed into it.

One primary advantage that hydroponics offer over traditional crop husbandry methods is that when the systems are carefully manipulated and the growing environment properly managed, in terms of the quantity of water provided, pH levels and the combination and concentration of the nutrients. When these conditions are looked into carefully, the crops grow faster. There is less waste in regard to the consumption of resources. There is also less reliance on fertilizers, pesticides and other potentially harmful products used in conventional agriculture.

This book covers the following topics:
- Introduction to hydroponics
- Advantages and disadvantages of hydroponics
- Terminology used in hydroponics
- Equipment/things you'll need

- Hydroponic grow systems
- How to select the best plants
- Pest and disease control
- Common mistakes made and how to avoid them

...And much more.

The development of hydroponics has not only been a response to the current food and resource problems. It is a solution for the future too. Experts say that by 2050, about 80% of all the food produced will be consumed in the cities, which makes it important for the cities to become producers of food. Currently, most cities are the good 'black holes' because all they do is suck in much of it, and at the same time, the cities are the biggest food wasters.

It is easy to see the wastefulness and excessive nature of normal food production in comparison to hydroponics. To supply food to the urban areas, producers need to produce it in large amounts and to transport it there, sometimes, across vast distances, before it is introduced into the market. From the initial step of production, harvesting, packaging, and shipping, the food takes up large amounts of resources that could be saved and re-used elsewhere.

People are involved, pollution-causing fuels, buildings, and other resources, and this is wasteful, in comparison to what hydroponics entails.

As the world's population is getting close to 7.5 billion and the demand for more food increasing just as fast, with emphasis on resource-intensive foods, it is clear that farming needs to be done even in the cities, and even so, more productively.

Ready to get started?

Richard Jones

Introduction

Hydroponics is a process where water is distributed, making sure to preserve the quality, and still provide the nutrients that the plants need to reach their full potential. This basically includes adding in some nutrients that the plants will need to the water that you provide them with, so the soil is not important. When you plant your produce in your garden, you are relying on the rain to help out with the process. The dirt is going to have a lot of the nutrients that your plants need in order to be strong and healthy. But the plants are not able to get all this goodness out on their own. Rather, the process waits for the rain to come, which then releases the nutrients and gives these to the plants. But when rain doesn't come, or you don't water your plants, you are not only dehydrating the plants, but you are keeping the nutrients in the soil away from the plants.

While this may seem like an easy process for the plants to get their nutrients, it is not perfect. There are times when there isn't enough rain. The soil may not have enough of the nutrients in it at all due to regional conditions and the plants can't thrive because of this lack of nutrients.

Or perhaps the nutrients are too far down in the soil for the water to be of sufficient help. No matter what the reason, this can make it really hard to provide the plant with the nutrients that it needs.

Since the natural way of providing nutrients to the plants is not always as effective as we may hope, hydroponics is sometimes used to overcome this anomaly. The goal of this process is to do a replication of the natural setting, but it is designed to make this work better. The way that this is done is by adding nutrients into the water and helping it to enrich the plants in the process. When the right nutrients are in the water, the plants are able to absorb them and grow healthier and stronger. If you do this process right, the plants will be able to grow better than they would in your own garden or another spot outside.

The nutrient solution is often up to you to create. You will usually need to make an enclosed system in order to move those nutrients around to the right place. The enclosed options used in hydroponics are great because they can also avoid the issue of evaporation so the plants can get all of the nutrients without the water evaporating.

The water will always be there, and you don't have to worry about the nutrients getting lost in the soil or that the water will disappear before all of the nutrients are absorbed. This method is super-efficient and puts you in control of feeding your plants the goodness they need.

There are a few different ways that you can set up your hydroponics. These are man-made so there are different choices and you will need to pick the one that is right for your garden, such as taking into account the size of growing area that you want and the right kinds of plants to suit your needs. You may want to look up a few plants to see what is available and which ones you will be able to get into the space you have available. Planning is everything.

Why Hydroponics?

Have you noticed lately that vegetables in supermarkets are missing something? It's all flavor. As with many industrial foods, the taste was substituted for consumer convenience.

Large-scale farming and marketing do, of course, provide the world's burgeoning population with vast quantities of food, but it is important to remember that quality suffers whenever quantity is stressed. As a result, your meals' flavor and nutritional value are reduced.

The varieties of seeds produced for "agribusiness" are one major reason for these declines. These seeds are selected for fast growth and high yield. The resulting vegetables and fruits have rugged skins for processing, storage, and shipping devices. Flavor and price are secondary concerns. Also, many vegetables are harvested unripe, particularly tomatoes, to ensure safe shipment and longer shelf life in the market. In fact, attempts are now being made to develop a hybrid square tomato that fits in packages.

More often than not, cities and villages grew up in frontier days, where farmers till the soil. They were good farmers and had the best soil to choose from. These towns and villages are our present day cities, still expanding and still engulfing valuable agricultural land.

As prime agricultural land disappears, as the costs of growers continue to rise, as transport costs increase in parallel with energy supplies, and as supermarket boards of directors become increasingly concerned with profit margins, we will see our food costs rise to the point of absurdity. World War II's Victory Gardens have been planted to raise unavailable food, and it seems realistic to say millions of people will use hydroponics in the near future to supply themselves with affordable vegetables and herbs of a quality that stores cannot match.

Introduction to Hydroponics

Hydroponics is the craft of growing plants without utilizing soil. To do this, hydroponics gear, by and large, comprises of a supply which contains nutrients, and some gadget which conveys this supplement answer for the plants. Farmers can utilize a wide range of development mediums wherein to put the plants. Rather than using soil, for instance, numerous plant specialists will use Rockwool, rock, sand, or even coco coir. In contrast to soil, which supplies nutrients to the underlying roots of the plants, these development mediums give room and backing to the roots to develop. Consequently, these mediums should be inactive.

Hydroponics is well known because it has various remarkable preferences for the cultivator. As a matter of first importance, it sets aside cash by enabling the farmer to reuse any water that is utilized. What's more, since the nutrients are assimilated more successfully, and controlled entirely by the planter, the expense of manure is boundlessly decreased. What's more, the yields of plants developed in hydroponics are steady and for the most part, very high.

Maybe the best bit of leeway of hydroponics is the way that it very well may be developed inside, which implies that your gardening is never again constrained by the season in which you decide to build it. In this way, even in the center of winter, you can develop plants that are sound and solid.

What is the reason why plants cultivated with hydroponics grow quicker than plants that don't utilize it?

Fundamentally, hydroponics gives the plant precisely what it needs when it needs it. This implies your plants can develop at the quickest speed that their hereditary qualities permit. When compared to plants grown in a standard, soil-based condition, hydroponically cultivated plants grow at a lot faster rate and frequently seem more beneficial.

How troublesome is it to utilize hydroponics hardware?

The viability of hydroponics hardware relies upon the expertise of the planter. If you can find the right pH, growing medium and hydroponic system, you could be surprised at the outcomes. That being stated, hydroponics hardware isn't tough to utilize. Necessary information on the equipment, joined with a touch of relevant knowledge, will be sufficient to fulfill the needs of any aspiring hydroponic farmer. All the fundamental knowledge that you require you can find it in this book.

For many individuals, securing the information to develop the best plants utilizing hydroponics is one of the most intriguing aspects of gardening. In case you're hoping to evaluate elective gardening strategies that are intended to show premium outcomes, hydroponics may be the ideal answer for you.

Plants for Hydroponic Gardening

We know what each of the hydroponic garden setups are, how we make several of our own and what kind of operation cycle we can expect to be going through. In this chapter, we are going to take a look at the different plants that are available for us to grow. We will take a brief look at each plant to get an idea of how they best grow in our hydroponic setups. From there we will be looking at the nutrition that our plants require.

Vegetables

When it comes to vegetables, there are a ton of options available to us. We'll be looking at a handful of these but first, let's tackle some general rules of thumb.

First up are those vegetables that grow underneath the soil. These are vegetables like onions, carrots and potatoes. These plants can still be grown in a hydroponic system, but they require extra work compared to those that grow above the surface like lettuce, cabbage and beans. This means that those under-the-soil plants require a little more advanced skill, and you may want to get some experience with your hydroponic system before you try to tackle them.

The other rule of thumb is that we should try to avoid crops like corn and zucchini and anything that relies on growing lots of vines. These types of plants take up a ton of space and just aren't very practical crops for hydroponic systems. Instead of focusing on a plant type that isn't practical, we can make better use of our space and systems.

Fruits

Nothing tastes sweeter than fruit that you have grown yourself. Hydroponic gardening offers a great way to grow some fruit inside the comfort of your own house. Like vegetables, there are many options available to us, but we'll be focusing on those that grow the best.

Herbs

Herbs make a great addition to any hydroponic setup. This is because it has been shown that herbs grown hydroponically have twenty to forty percent more aromatic oils than herbs that have been grown in a traditional soil garden. This means that you get more out of your hydroponic herbs with less used. This allows you to use less for the same end goal in your cooking, which means that your herbs will last you longer.

The best system for growing herbs is the ebb and flow system. Hydroponic herb gardens have been becoming a norm across the world because of their effectiveness. There are now even restaurants that grow their own hydroponic herb gardens on site because it is the most effective way to get fresh herbs of amazing quality.

Basil is the most popular of the herbs, with basil making up about 50% of the herb market in Europe. Both basil and mint like a warm environment and a pH level between 5.5 and 6.5. Similarly, chives prefer a warm to hot temperature and a pH sitting squarely around 6.0. This means that if you are careful with the temperature and pH level you can grow all three of these wonderful herbs in the same hydroponic setup.

An herb garden is a great way to get started with hydroponics. They can stay harvestable for incredibly long periods of time; they taste better than herbs grown in soil and make great additions to just about any meal. Not only that but herb gardens tend to be smaller than vegetable or fruit gardens and so a hydroponic herb garden will take up less space and can save some money in setup costs.

Hydroponics - Historical Background

The growing of plants in plant nutrient component abundant water has been practiced for a considerable length of time. For instance, the old Hanging Gardens of Babylon and the drifting nurseries of the Aztecs in Mexico were hydroponic. During the 1800s, the fundamental ideas for the hydroponic growth of plants were set up by those examining how plants develop.
The soilless culture of plants was then advanced during the 1930s in a progression of distributions by a California researcher.

During the Second World War, the US Army built up huge hydroponic cultivates on a few islands in the western Pacific to supply crisp vegetables to troops working around there.

Since the 1980s, the hydroponic procedure has come into business use for vegetable and bloom production, with more than 86,000 sections of land of nursery vegetables being developed hydroponically all through the world, a real estate that is relied upon to keep on expanding.

One of the parts of hydroponics that has impacted its conventions is the way that the hydroponic strategy for growing plants is used primarily in controlled conditions, for example, nurseries, where the air encompassing plants and its temperature, humidity, and development are controlled. Indeed, even the effect of sunlight-based radiation is fairly controlled (modified) by the transmission attributes of the nursery glazing.

In this manner, those writing about their utilization of a specific hydroponic method are mentioning objective facts that are the consequence of the connection between the plant condition and growing procedure, regardless of whether it is a (flood-and-drain) NFT or drip water system method with plants rooted in Rockwool or Coir sections, or basins.

Then, the inquiry concerns the estimation of Information being accounted for when plants are developed in a glass nursery located in the mountains of Arizona utilizing the Rockwool chunk drip water system for somebody who might be mulling overgrowing a similar plant-animal varieties in a twofold polyethylene-shrouded nursery situated in the waterfront fields of south Georgia (United States) utilizing the Rockwool piece drip-water system growing method. From one's genuine experience, the study of hydroponics ought to be characterized depending on going with environmental conditions; that one lot of hydroponic growing strategies would just apply to a specific arrangement of growing parameters and consequently not a fixed arrangement of techniques that would apply all around. Until this is comprehended, the utilization of the hydroponic method of growing will wallow in a labyrinth of misinformation; growers will be continually scanning for answers to why things happened as they managed without revealing the reason, and the individuals who need to realize the reason will be searching for an answer in all inappropriate spots.

Legitimate guidance in the plan and functions of a hydroponic culture system is significant.

Those curious about the potential risks related to these systems or who neglect to understand the science of the nutrient solution required for their legitimate administration and plant nourishment will not make business progress with most hydroponic culture systems.

The innovation related to hydroponic plant production has changed a little, as can be seen by auditing the different book references on hydroponics. Today, those keen on hydroponics look for Information from sites on the Internet. The test isn't an absence of Information (there are more than 400,000 hydroponic sites), yet rather the flood of Information, much inadequate with regards to a scientific premise, that prompts disarray and poor basic leadership concerning clients.

The study of hydroponics is presently least examined, and a significant part of the present spotlight is on the utilization of existing hydroponic techniques. Hydroponics is characterized as a method of growing crops; it is, in effect, principally supported by those in the private part who have a personal stake in its financial improvement depending on the products that they showcase.

The job that business and scientific headways have on society can't be overlooked when thinking about what is happening in hydroponics today. The simplicity of the development of products by surface and air transport, for instance, takes into account growing food products at significant stretches from their place of utilization.

The appearance of plastics has enormously affected hydroponics because growing vessels, fluid stockpiling tanks, drip irrigation tubing and fittings, nursery coating materials, and sheeting materials basic segments in all hydroponic/nursery operations are gotten from a wide scope of plastic materials that differ in their physical and chemical attributes.

The utilization of PCs and PC control of virtually every part of a hydroponic/nursery activity has reformed basic leadership and administrative control techniques. Albeit one may presume that hydroponic crop production is turning out to be increasingly more scientific, there is still a lot of workmanship necessitated that makes this method of plant production a test just as an experience.

How Plants Develop

The antiquated scholars pondered about how plants develop. They presumed that plants got sustenance from the soil, considering it a specific juice existent in the soil for use by plants. In the sixteenth century, van Helmont viewed water as the sole nutrient for plants. He arrived at this resolution in the wake of leading the accompanying test: growing a willow in an enormous deliberately gauged tub of soil. In contrast, the willow expanded in weight from 5 to 169 pounds. Since only water was added to the soil, he presumed that plant growth was caused exclusively by water.

Later in the sixteenth century, John Woodward developed spearmint in different sorts of water and saw that growth expanded with expanding pollution of the water. He inferred that plant growth grew in water that contained expanding measures of the earthbound issue because this issue is deserted in the plant as water goes through the plant.

The possibility that soil water conveyed food for plants and that plants live off the soil, commanded the thinking about the times. It was not until the mid to late eighteenth century that experimenters started plainly to understand how, surely, plants develop. At about a similar time, the humus hypothesis of plant growth was proposed and generally acknowledged. The idea hypothesized that plants get carbon (C) and fundamental nutrients (components) from soil humus. This was most likely the main proposal of what might today be known as the natural gardening (cultivating), idea of plant growth and prosperity. Trials and perceptions made by numerous individuals from that point forward have limited the fundamental reason for the humus hypothesis that plant health comes just from soil humus sources.

Hydroponic Practice and the Craft of Hydroponics

Any individual who wishes to try hydroponics has prepared access to every one of the assets that should have been fruitful and can develop plants utilizing one of the different hydroponic growing systems with great outcomes. The test is to take those equivalent assets and complete guide for growing vegetables; the crop produces the most noteworthy plant yield and quality.

Strolling into any nursery wherein plants are being developed hydroponically, I can rapidly evaluate the nature of the board aptitude being applied, the aftereffect of applying one of a kind ability that a few people appear to have that capacity to take a lot of operational parameters and make them work viably and effectively together. I am one who solidly accepts that there are people who have what is known as a green thumb, while there are other people who do well, yet they seem to remain at a level of execution underneath those with a green thumb. It is like the individuals who can prepare a tasty supper, while another person utilizing similar data sources can generate a gourmet feast.

Hydroponics Is a Useful Technique

Hydroponics is exceptionally profitable; it is a technique that moderates water and land. It is additionally ok for nature. Hydroponics is cutting edge; however, it requires just fundamental horticultural abilities in the first place.

It is imperative to manage air and root temperatures among different elements like light, water, plant nutrition, and extraordinary atmospheres.

Hence, hydroponics systems should frequently work in temperature-controlled situations like nurseries.

Hydroponics is a type of soilless culture where plants are developed in different arrangements, with or without the utilization of a medium. Hydroponics is greatly beneficial; it is a growing technique that does not need huge amount of water and land. It is additionally beneficial for nature. Hydroponics gardening is innovative. However, it requires sufficient knowledge before one can start. It is imperative to control air and root temperatures among different elements like light, water, plant nutrition, and extraordinary atmospheres. Thus, hydroponics systems should frequently work in temperature-controlled conditions like nurseries. It is essential to consider the nursery conditions else; hydroponics will quit being savvy for you.

In fluid hydroponics systems, there is no supporting mechanism for the plant roots. This is otherwise called arrangement culture; the three primary sorts of arrangement culture are arrangement culture, constant stream arrangement culture, and aeroponics. Plants are developed in compartments of hydroponic supplement arrangement. They are generally home-level applications where hydroponics systems work in glass containers, plastic basins, tubs, and tanks.

Advantages and Disadvantages of Hydroponics

Advantages of Hydroponics

Farming and gardening techniques are changing and improving, much like technology. The soil-less technique or hydroponics is quickly becoming popular because it gives farmers and gardeners less to worry about.

Hydroponics allows plants to grow in nutrient solutions instead of soil that leaves tilling, weeding, fertilizing, pesticide spraying and cultivation out of the picture. Moreover, bigger crop results can be achieved in shorter amounts of time. It is an easy and more efficient way to grow vegetables, fruits and flowers. In addition, the produce is healthier and contains more nutrient value.

Hydroponic gardens can be maintained indoors and outdoors and are very undemanding and inexpensive to maintain.

Here are some key advantages to using hydroponic systems:
- Garden anywhere. Hydroponic gardens require no soil. You can practice hydroponics in any given place. You do not have to worry if you don't possess a basement or a yard. You can comfortably use a tabletop system placed in your room and manage to grow some wonderful fresh crops. So even if you live in an area where soil quality is poor, your plants will thrive. Crops can be grown in greenhouses and even in desert regions.
- Hydroponic gardens require less land surface. Plants can be grown in mediums that can be placed in high-density areas or multi-story buildings. The hydro units can also be stacked.
- Hydroponic gardening ensures a high yield in a controlled environment. The needed nutrient environment can be maintained and provided to ensure plant growth and productivity. Compared to soil cultures, a small space can produce up to about ten times the size of plant matter. You have better plans as well. Since you have complete control over your plant's nutritional needs, you can grow them to

the best of their ability. You know your plant has enough of everything to grow bigger and better than any soil version could. You'll have a higher yield because your plant is healthier and can physically produce more.

- Hydroponics promotes water conservation. Plants are given the accurate amount of water that they need. If you grow plants in soil, you will require 90% more water to nourish the plant compared to a properly designed hydroponics system. Labor for watering is also avoided as the water stays in the hydroponic system. Since hydroponics actually uses 2/3 less water than conventional farming, it means you're recirculating the water and not letting it run off. This also means that if there is ever an accident and the water become hazardous, it's also not simply running into the local environment and damaging the ecosystem like traditional farming methods often does. This also means it's not as expensive since you're not using as much water or as many nutrients because they are subject to recirculation and it's more efficient.

- Hydroponic gardens and farms can be set up in places with cheap water and power. When established in close proximity to places where there is a high demand for a particular crop, transport and shipping costs are reduced.
- Hydroponic gardening eliminates the need for pesticide and herbicide. It is possible to go organic with this set-up. Likewise, it is easier to eliminate plant diseases and pests.
- Hydroponic gardening ensures that there is no nutrition pollution to the environment. Aeration is made possible and the risk of calcium, potassium, and phosphorus run-off is easily prevented.
- Hydroponic gardeners and farmers do not have to mulch, weed, till and change the soil. They also don't need to add fertilizer to the soil, and it is also easy to harvest crops.
- Grow Year Round. Thanks to be an indoor project you're not limited by the time of year. Many temperate or even arid climates will not support farming outside year-round. This means that you can grow fresh crops year-round without being at the

whim of Mother Nature and it also means your crops are safe from environmental disasters like river pollution and acid rain.
- It is enjoyable. Soil farming is backbreaking work. Whether it's kneeling down to put plants in or tilling soil traditional gardening means physical work. Since you're not doing any of these things and your plants are grown at table height you can enjoy it more. It's also a great scientific method that provides an interesting project for the whole family. Most kids hate getting into the garden but tell them to start mixing solutions that change color and monitoring things to see how they grow, and it becomes much more interactive.

Disadvantages of Hydroponics

There are many benefits to hydroponic gardening. Lack of land, a frequent supply of water and other environmental concerns can be conquered with hydroponics. With the right knowledge and proper techniques, it is a valuable system for commercial farmers and gardeners.

Despite the fact that there's plenty of reasons to choose hydroponics many shy away from this "new" technology just because it's unfamiliar or because of the stigmatic connection with cannabis growing. The major factor for most individuals is that the initial investment is costly. Dirt is simply cheap, especially when compared to grow beds, special monitors, lighting, and the time needed to get everything running right. A large system is especially daunting as no one wants to make that sort of investment and then find it's not going to work for them.

For one, the initial cost to set-up a properly designed and effective hydroponic system is high. In the long run, the conservation of water and nutrients may prove to be inexpensive but before you can enjoy those benefits, you need to set-up a hydroponic system with all the necessary equipment. Hydroponic equipment does not come cheap. Additionally, technical knowledge and skills are required to maintain the equipment.

Other disadvantages of hydroponic garden systems are the following:

1. Compared to farming in large fields, hydroponic gardening may yield a limited production.

2. Hydroponic gardening requires constant supervision. You need to be responsible and diligent because the plants depend on you for their survival.
3. If you have insufficient knowledge, you will depend on trial and error. Some plants will flourish while others may die. You should be prepared to encounter frustrations and disappointments.
4. Hydroponic gardens are interrupted and influenced by power outages and pump failures.
5. Because there is no soil to act as a buffer, the plant will wither and die rapidly once the system fails. If interruptions occur, the plants must be watered manually.
6. Should a water-borne organism or disease appear in your set-up, it will quickly spread, and all plants will be easily affected. Hence, vegetative growth and production are disturbed.
7. As with any project, make sure you consider all aspects and count the costs before you decide to set-up your own hydroponic system.

Terminology Used In Hydroponics

Learning and mastering hydroponics can be overwhelming especially with all the terms you may encounter in the long run. There is usually too much information making it difficult for beginners to determine a solid base where they can start. Let's discuss these terms as simple as possible.

Air Pump

This is optional in other hydroponic systems aside deep-water culture system. Using an air pump is beneficial and relatively cheap. It helps in supplying oxygen and air in the water.

In deep water culture systems, the air pumps prevent the plants from suffocation while they are drenched with the nutrient solution. For other types of systems, it aids in increasing the level of dissolved oxygen. It keeps the water oxygenated by producing air bubbles. It also enables circulation of the nutrients and helps in reducing pathogens.

Air Stone

Whilst this is not an essential composition of a hydroponic system, an air stone is highly recommended to use. It is ideal in adding oxygen to the nutrient solution. It promotes faster growth of the plants and keeps the solution fresher.

Germination

At the point when a seed initially starts to grow, it is sprouting. Seeds are developed in a growing medium, for example, Perlite. A few elements are engaged with this procedure. To start with, the seed must be dynamic, and alive, and not in torpidity. Most seeds have a specific temperature go that must be accomplished. Moisture and oxygen must be available. And, for certain seeds, specified degrees of light or dimness must be achieved.

Grow Lights

A supplemental light is highly required for an indoor hydroponic grow box. The plant needs 10-12 hours of light daily for optimal growth. Set the light hanging over the top of your plants with a distance of about 6 inches from the top point of it. Adjust the lights as your plant gets taller to avoid damaging or burning the leaves. Prolonged light exposure can also damage the roots and gives heat stress to the plants.

As a beginner, you can do a homemade hydroponic system using the resources at home. You must also consider the space of your grow area, the holding tank or reservoir and room overhead for the lighting system. Start by planting veggies or herbs which are easier to manage to test the efficiency of your system. Make changes or adapt new strategies to become a successful grower.

Growing Medium

Basically, this is where you are letting your plant grows. In soil gardening, soil is the medium used and in hydroponics, various materials can be used to support the root systems and weight of the plants.

All plants require some medium or another for the plants to thrive. In the hydroponics system, although water is the primary medium, it still requires soil, perlite, etc. to support the plants and help the roots absorb and retain the nutrients. You can choose any of these or lava, rock, etc. You must pick the medium based on the type of plants that you have. Some plants do well in soil while some in perlite etc.

Growing Tray or Chamber

This will hold the entire plant especially the root zone. It can be made of plastic materials, a container, an old huge tray or anything that can keep your growing plants and provides support. You can use almost any containers for the grow chamber but avoid anything that is made of metal as it may have negative reactions with the nutrient solution.

The container should be filled with plenty of holes for a better flow of water. Apparently, the size of the grow tray will depend on the size and type of hydroponic system you will be using and the plants you will be growing. Bigger plants have huge root systems, so they need bigger space to hold them.

Hydroponics technique

There are many hydroponics techniques to pick from, and you can choose whatever fits your budget the best. Although the NFT remains the most popular hydroponics system, you can choose any other as well and ask for a demonstration so that you can decide on the best one. Once you have the right technique, you can look for brands that supply the best equipment to kick-start your hydroponics journey.

When it comes to the equipment needed to set up the hydroponics garden, you can either choose a readymade set or look for different parts that can be assembled. The materials need to be high quality and bought from trusted dealers.

Look online for discounts. Once you get the materials, inspect them to make sure they are good quality before setting up the garden.

Make sure everything is working well and will not create problems once you set up your hydroponics garden.

Insects and Diseases

Check for plant insects and diseases that can affect plant health. Right from eggs to larvae, there can be many things that can infest your garden and reduce your plant's lifespan. You have to keep an eye on it and ensure that none of these negatively affects your plants and are kept away. Make use of a mild insecticide such as neem and a little boric powder but make sure you use them in the recommended quantities.

Monitoring

Keep an eye on the plants you have sown. You must check from time to time whether they are doing well. Check them at least two to three times a day so that you know how they are faring.

Check the growing medium, the pH level of water, nutrient quality etc. all these contribute towards ensuring that your garden flourishes and produce healthy blooms, fruits and vegetables year after year.

Nutrients

All plants require nutrients to grow healthy. Your hydroponic plants will need nutrients that are specifically meant to be used for the hydroponics garden and designed to help plants absorb the nutrition with ease. The nutrients have to be released slowly in small portions throughout the day. You have to make use of a timer to time the release of the nutrients into the water. These nutrients will leave you with bigger and more nutritious fruit and vegetables.

Nutrient Reservoir

Also called as reservoir, holds the nutrient solution before feeding the plants. It can be a large container made of plastic and an old fish tank that can hold plenty of water.

Keep in mind that the reservoir should not be made of metallic materials to avoid harmful elements to mix with the nutrient solution.

Nutrient Solution

This is probably the most vital part of any hydroponic system. While it may sound complicated, this is basically nutrients dissolved in water which made hydroponics a successful method of growing plants. It just not feed the plants with water but with nutrient-rich water that is essential for the plant's optimal growth. It can be in a form of soluble or in various mixes. We will go into details about nutrient solution as we proceed.

Most of the hydroponics systems keep the nutrient reservoir separate from the grow tray or chamber. For the plant to access the nutrient solution, the delivery system should be working efficiently to move the nutrient solution from its reservoir to the tray and drain the excess back to the reservoir.

Saplings and Seeds

You have to buy the seeds and the saplings that will be used to grow the garden. Look for high-quality seeds and saplings that are recommended for the hydroponics set up. Start out with herbs so that you get the hang of the way in which the garden works. You can then move on to fruits and vegetables. This book will give you a kick-start and teach you about a few plants that you can get started with.

Set Up

Obviously, you have to set up your garden. You must lay down the pipes, the reservoir, the growing medium should be added in, the plants should be planted, etc. The water and nutrients should flow through the systems properly so that your plants have the chance to receive them. In every setup, two pipes should attach to the reservoir, one inlet, and one outlet. There should also be a pump that adds in the air to the system.

If you are using the Aeroponics system, then you should buy sprinklers that will directly spray the water onto the roots of the plants.

You can ask the person at the store to help you out or find someone who can help you set up the systems. Once the systems have been set up, you can give it a trial to check if everything is working fine. If there is an issue, then fix it immediately.

Submersible Pump

A submersible pump or "pump" is featured in all hydroponics systems. This is often the same type of pump included in a normal aquarium set-up. It pumps the nutrient water from the reservoir to the grow tray. Aside from keeping the water oxygenated, it also discourages the growth of algae. The submersible pump comes in various shapes and sizes and is widely available in-home improvement shops.

Timer

Depending on the system you will use and its place in the garden, a simple set of timers is essential.

You will need this in setting the time of your artificial grow light to control the lighting system. For hydroponic systems such as aeroponics, drip and ebb and flow, a time is essential in controlling the submersible pump.

Hydroponic Growing Systems

There are hundreds of methods of hydroponic gardening. However, all these are combinations or variations of six basic types:

1. Water Culture
2. Wicks
3. Nutrient Film Techniques
4. Flood and Drains
5. Drips
6. Aeroponics

The following paragraphs give descriptions of the basic hydroponic systems and details how each of them works.

The Water Culture System

The Water Culture System is the simplest form of active hydroponics.

The plants are commonly grown on a medium made of Styrofoam and they grow directly from the nutrient solution. This system uses an air pump to supply oxygen to the plants' roots.

The Water Culture System is the best choice for growing water-loving plants such as lettuce. However, this system is not suitable for many long term or large plants, and these will not thrive using this system.

It is not expensive to make this type of hydroponic system. You can use an old aquarium or water container. It is the ideal set-up for a classroom. This makes it a popular choice for teachers and students.

The Wick System

Wicking is the simplest form of passive hydroponics. Passive means there are no moving parts in the system. The nutrient solution comes up through the wick from the reservoir and feeds the growing medium through this wick.

The growing mediums used for this system are coconut fiber, pro-mix, vermiculite and perlite. It is an effective system for small plants because large plants tend to draw up the nutrient solution faster than the wicks can supply them.

Nutrient Film Technique

The Nutrient Film Technique or NFT is the most prevalent type of hydroponics. It is probably the cheapest and easiest to create. The benefit of this system is that no soil is used.

The roots of the plants are suspended directly in water and the nutrient solution is pumped into the water that covers the roots and drained back into a reservoir.

There is no need for a timer, and you do not have to replace the growing medium after every change of crop. The NFT usually makes use of a small plastic basket that has been designed to let the roots dangle into the nutrient solution. The only drawback is that when power outages and pump failures occur, the flow of solution is interrupted, and the roots tend to dry out easily.

The Flood and Drain System

This is known as the "Ebb and Flow." It works by flooding the growing medium or tray with the nutrient solution and draining it back to the reservoir. This action is achieved by a submersible pump, which is connected to a pre-set timer.

The timer will trigger the pump to siphon the nutrient solution onto the tray. After this action, the timer will also shut the pump off so that the solution will ebb back. The gardener will set the timer to turn on several times during the day – the frequency will be dependent on several factors:

- Type of plant
- Size of plant
- Temperature
- Humidity
- Growing medium

The grow tray can be filled with different growing mediums. The most popular choices are Rockwool, perlite, gravel, coconut fiber and grow rocks. Most people use individual pots as trays.

The main challenge with the "Ebb and Flow" system is the susceptibility to power outages, pump failures, and timer failures. Some mediums like gravel and grow rocks will not hold the nutrient solution well enough so the roots will dry out quickly when the cycle is interrupted. It is better to use Rockwool, coconut fiber, and pro-mix as they retain more water.

Drip System (Recovery / Non-Recovery System)

The Drip System is the most widely used hydroponic system. It is set-up with a timer, a submerged pump, and a grow tray. The timer is set to turn the pump on to allow the nutrient solution to drip off directly onto the plants through a tiny drip line.

There are two kinds of Drip Systems: Recovery and Non-Recovery. In a Recovery Drip, the surplus nutrient solution that flows down is collected in a reservoir and re-used. In a Non-Recovery Drip, the nutrient solution that runs off is not collected.

The Recovery Drip System is more efficient and less expensive. Apart from being able to re-use the excess nutrient solution, the system does not need precise control for the watering cycles. The timer needs to be more precise in a Non-Recovery Drip System, so the plants get enough of the nutrient solution and there is minimal runoff.

The Recovery System requires more maintenance in recycling the solution back to the reservoir and the pH and strength of the nutrient solution needs to be preserved.

This requires periodic testing and adjusting so that pH and strength levels do not shift. On the other hand, the Non-Recovery System needs less maintenance, as the solution is not re-used.

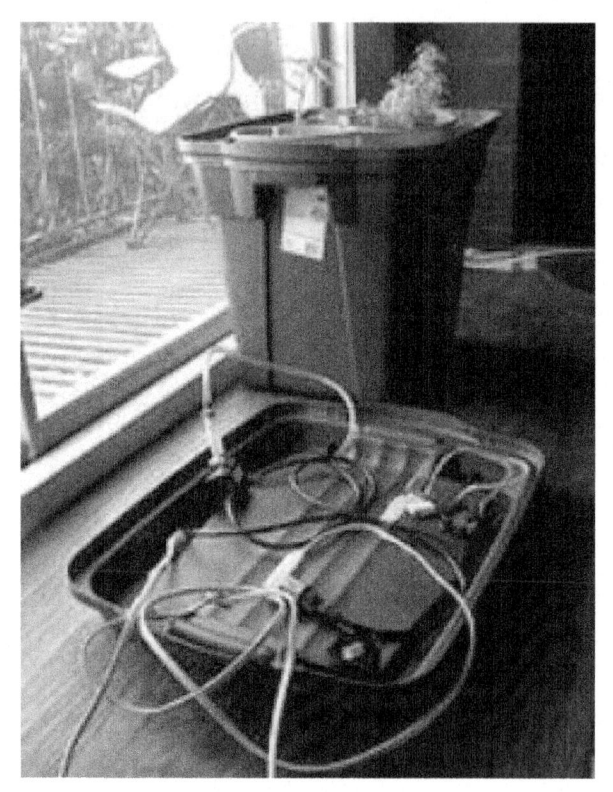

Aeroponics

This is the one of the high-tech systems in hydroponic gardening. The growing medium for the aeroponic system is air. The plants' roots are misted with the nutrient solution every few minutes.

A timer triggers the misting pump, similar to on the other hydroponic systems. The only difference is that there is a shorter cycle for the pump.

It is a quite delicate and complicated system. There should be no interruption to misting cycles. Otherwise, the roots will dry out quickly.

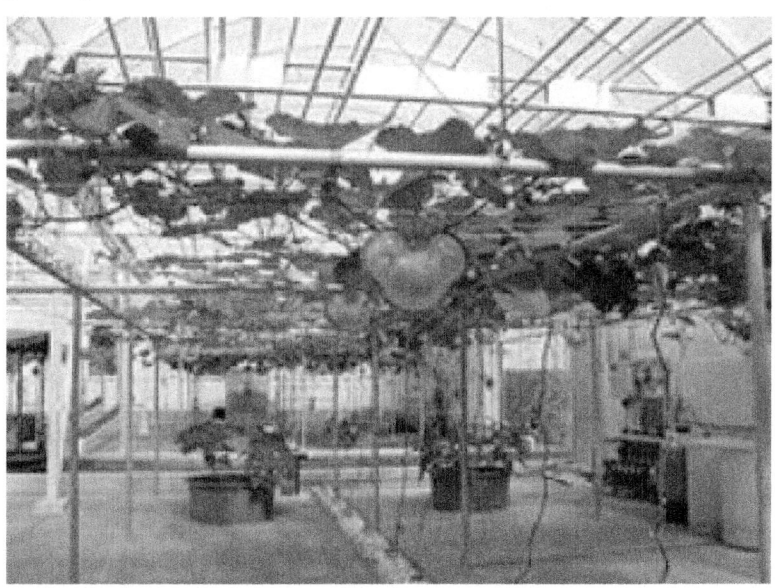

Choosing Which Hydroponic Setup Is Right for You

There are many types of hydroponic systems, each with its advantages and disadvantages. Different plants often need various systems. For example, if one wanted to grow strawberries, because of the small root systems, one would use a nutrient film technology setup. But if you wanted to make tomatoes, you would like to use a system that gives you much greater root growth, like deep water or ebb & flow.

Deep water cultivation systems are generally known as the easiest and cheapest hydroponic installations. Deep water culture systems are characterized by roots directly submerged in a water / nutrient reservoir, with air stones preserving the oxygenation of the body. These systems often do not have the same rate of growth as complicated systems as aeroponics. If you are just beginning with hydroponics, this is an excellent choice.

Nutrient film technical systems for smaller crops like lettuce and strawberries are commonly used. They are costlier than deep water culture as they need a water pump to flow water from the reservoir via either PVC pipes or a similar rising container. Such systems have good growth levels because of their high root oxygen exposure.

Aeroponics is considered the most complex hydroponic device, but also the one with the highest growth rates. These systems work by misting the root systems and providing much higher absorption of oxygen and nutrients. Aeroponics should only be attempted by someone who has already installed many hydroponic systems.

Hydroponics On A Budget

While hydroponic gardening may seem to be a complicated and expensive enterprise, it is very affordable as more people grow indoor plants, and the supplies they need are becoming affordable. It's become more expensive to buy food in food shops and growing things like vegetables indoors is a fantastic idea to save money and eat healthier at the same time.

All varieties of tomatoes and courgettes can be grown indoors and used to make a healthy and cost-effective meal.

Hydroponics has long been around, and the technology has, over time, been streamlined and improved to produce an inexpensive and convenient tool. Several stores and blogs have given recommendations for hydroponic growth methods to produce desirable results repeatedly, which are easy to understand. The main aspect of successfully growing with a hydroponic system is to use tried and true techniques consistently. The basic supplies that you need include a nutrient solution, pH strips, adequate lighting, and seeds that generate anything that you create.

The average hydroponic configuration can be bought for around $150.00 and easily maintained with little or no maintenance. It is a good idea to keep alert on your plants, but with the wonders of the hydroponics, you don't have to worry about them getting sufficient nutrients from the soil because nutrients come from a liquid solution. Just be sure to check your system's pH level on a regular basis to ensure that your plants are not harmed. Due diligence is the name of the game for hydroponic systems and includes knowledge of the growth cycle of your plant.

An ideal method for beginners is the nutrient film technique in which only a very small amount of water is poured over the roots of the plants so they can also quickly absorb oxygen. This method helps to accelerate plant growth and ensure a healthy life with time. This is an excellent method for novices and professionals, but the low water level ensures that the water height and pH are more closely tracked. It is a good idea to know what the root structure of your plant is about when you set up it will not be nice if the roots are too long.

As the economy continues to suffer from home gardening globally, many could and will probably become a way of life in view of its inherent benefits. However, growing food is not the only thing that grows at home. Those who live in US states where legal, medical marijuana can grow their own medicine. This greatly reduces prices, and in some countries, the finished product can even legally be sold to your local dispensary.

Hydroponics Growing — Beyond Theory

The perception that only expert gardeners should try the process is one of the great myths of hydroponics growing.

Sadly, this misconception has spread over the years, despite being far from the facts. The growth of hydroponics is so quick that anyone ambitious enough to learn the techniques can do this with a minimum of effort.

It is important to note that some effort is required to start growing hydroponics, but not much talent, only ambition. You don't have to be master gardener, if you're not a great gardener, to grow fruit and vegetables effectively by hydroponic methods; perhaps you'll have to try to kill your plants if you're not a great gardener.

The best way of starting with hydroponic growth for uninitiated is to take as much information on the field as possible and then to dirty their hands and start planting for themselves. This is quite an important point; if you want to learn hydroponics, you have to start hydroponics. Homemade Hydroponics offers an amazing online training course that teaches you the basic and advanced techniques needed to grow hydroponically successfully and to start creating your hydroponic equipment so that you can grow your food and test new techniques. It is certainly not a theory-based course, it is a practical one, and it's dirty to get people up and run with their hydroponic gardens. This is the perfect way to start with what can be a very satisfying and potentially delicious hobby.

Equipment & Things You'll Need

In this chapter you are going to learn about all of the components that are needed in order to grow plants using a hydroponic system. It is crucial to understand that each and every component of your hydroponic system is equally important. Without a fully operational and proper component, the other components will not be effective.

Here is a look at some of the things you must decide upon before getting started with the hydroponics garden. Make sure you buy all good quality products so that your garden thrives.

Atmosphere Controls

Present-day nurseries employ propelled condition control helps, for example, transfers, humidistats, indoor regulators CO_2 infusion systems, and fans, which are regularly constrained by a focal PC. Littler systems employ different individual control units.

Automatic Timer

Automatic timers are used to release water into the garden, releasing nutrients into the water, etc. Timers play a huge role in keeping your plants healthy. You must buy a timer that is of good quality and will work well throughout the year.

You can also opt for a manual timer, but it will require you to switch it off and back on every day at the same time, which can prove to be a hassle. Automatic timers are more reliable and more comfortable to operate and can last you longer.

Grow Lights

Grow lights are essential when it comes to growing plants using the hydroponics system. Grow lights help grow plants normally in the absence of sunlight. Grow lights are designed to help plants prepare their foods and grow normally. You must use stronger grow lights for those plants that require 10 to 12 straight hours of sun and lighter ones for those that require lesser hours of sun. You must pay attention to the quality of the grow lights and make sure that you buy only high-quality ones as otherwise you will end up compromising on plant health. Good quality lights might be a little expensive compared to low-quality ones but will last you long and help you grow healthy plants.

Here are some grow lights to consider.

LED lights

LED lights are great for growing indoor plants. People who grow marijuana indoors mostly use them. Cannabis plants thrive under LED lights and can be used to grow healthy plants. LED lights can either be full spectrum lights or single lights. Multi-spectrum lights come in handy when you wish to grow plants that are at different stages of growth. LED lights make a good choice as their lifespan ranges between 20,000 and 100,000 hours.

This is quite high for grow bulbs. But most LED lights are quite expensive and can cost anywhere between $100 and $1000.

Fluorescent bulbs

Fluorescent bulbs are usually used for plants that have just started sprouting. They are quite mild and will suit a variety of plants all in different stages of growth. Fluorescent bulbs can be slightly less expensive than LED bulbs. They will not be suitable for all plants.

HID

High-intensity discharge lights are those that are used in grow rooms. They do not glow as brightly as LED ones but can last longer. They are suitable for a variety of plants and can last about 50,000 hours. Make sure you choose the right light to suit your plants. Remember that most lights heat up quite a bit and so you have to ensure that you make use of a fan to cool the plants down and prevent them from heating up too much and burning.

Growing Chamber

You will need a growing chamber or a growing tray. This will hold the set system. It can be made of any type of antithetical material. Most people use pots that can be found at any general retailer that is near you.

Growing Medium

Soil is never used in hydroponic growing. A few systems can boost the growing of plants, enabling the exposed roots to have most of the supplement arrangement. In different systems, the roots are upheld by a growing medium. A few sorts of media additionally help in moisture and supplement maintenance.

Different media are more qualified for specific plants and systems. It is ideal to look into the entirety of your alternatives and to get a few suggestions for systems and media before putting resources into or building activity. Well known growing media include:

- Composted bark. It is normally natural and can be used for seed germination.
- Expanded earth. Pellets are prepared in a hot stove, which causes them to expand, making a permeable finished result.
- Gravel. Any sort can be used. However, rock can add minerals to supplement. Continuously ensure it is spotless.

- Oasis. This artificial, froth-based material is usually referred to from its use as a course of action based in the flower business.
- Peat greenery. This medium is a carbonized and compacted vegetable tissue that has been somewhat disintegrated.
- Perlite. Volcanic Glass is mined from magma streams and warmed in heaters to a high temperature, causing the modest quantity of moisture inside to expand.
- Pumice. This is a smooth material that shaped by volcanic movement. Pumice is lightweight due to its enormous number of depressions delivered by the ejection of water fume at a high temperature as magma surfaces.
- Rockwool. This is made by liquefying rock at a high temperature and then turning it into strands.
- Sand. This medium shifts in structure and is generally used related to another medium.
- Vermiculite. Like Perlite, except for that, is has a moderately high trade limit, which means it can hold nutrients for later use.
- Various materials can (and are) used as growing medium. Hydroponic plant specialists will, in general be an inventive and test gathering.

Lighting and Heat

Photosynthesis is crucial to all plant life. It can only happen when their atmosphere is sufficiently warm. If the temperature falls too low or fluctuates through the day, the photosynthesis will be stunted or even not occur. The temperate conditions that the plant is accustomed to are a great effect on how the plants grow using a system. If the temperature is lower than what they are used too, then they will grow very slowly, this is the opposite of what you want to happen. Most plants will thrive at 65 degrees Fahrenheit, but not any lower. It is highly suggested to keep their environmental temperature at 70 – 75 degrees Fahrenheit.

Plants are used to temperatures dropping during the night a little bit, but do not allow it to drop too much. Do not allow it to fall below 50 degrees Fahrenheit. If you find that even though your plants are at the right temperature, if you find they are too warm, set them on the floor.

Location

First off, you must choose the right spot to have your hydroponics garden. The garden should be in a spot where it can thrive and grow in size. The space you choose has to be big enough for the pipes and reservoir to fit in and have enough space around to move. Remember that hydroponics garden can do well both indoors and outdoors. You have to pick a spot where it will be easier for the plants to receive the vital necessities to thrive such as light and proper aeration. If you are going to create an indoor garden, then you have to install lights that will act as grow lights and help your plants grow well. You might also require a dehumidifier and a fan to keep the plants cool.

Money

It is obvious that you will require money to set up the garden. You have to set aside a budget so that you can quickly set up your hydroponics garden. An average garden can cost anywhere between $100 and $500 depending on the size, the materials chosen and the plants that you wish to grow.

The budget must include the equipment to use, the seeds or saplings, the growing material, nutrients, etc. All these should be top quality so that you can have a healthy, flourishing garden.

Nutrients

Nutrients form an essential part of the hydroponics garden. You have to mix them in the right quantities and ensure that all plants receive the nutrients. Each plant requires a different nutrient, and so you must combine them in the right proportions. Once the nutrients have been mixed in, you must wait for at least 30 minutes before you add them to the plants. Make sure you keep an eye on the ph. level of water, as it is vital to maintain the right ph. levels to enhance plant growth. The temperature of the water should be ideal for the plants and not too hot or too cold as it can affect root health. Follow the instructions provided on the nutrient pack to mix them in the right proportions.

pH Meter

A pH meter is an absolute must when it comes to growing plants using the hydroponics system. The pH meter helps you test the ph. levels in the soil. Some plants require an acidic base while some need a neutral one.

You have to maintain the level of whatever is ideal for the plants and will only lead to an upkeep of their health and keep them from getting damaged. If the levels are too low or too high, then you can add a few solutions to bring back balance.

Plants

Choose the right plants to sow into the systems. Some plants do better than others and so, pick out the ones that are specifically designed to suit hydroponics. Different hydroponic systems suit different plants such as the NFT system suits fruits while the drip system is ideal for growing herbs. Pick the one based on the type of produce you wish to grow so that you can make the most of your hydroponics garden. Try to sow 5 to 6 at first and monitor them for a couple of months to check how they respond before going for more plants.

Pump Set

A pump set is required regardless of the hydroponics system that you are setting up.

Pumps help in pumping the water and nutrients into the system. Your plants will thrive if you choose a set that is good quality and pumps in the right amount of water. A pump set is also used to remove excess water from the system. Automatic pumps help in draining water efficiently and also letting it in. You will also need an air pump or an aeration pump that adds air into the system. You can pick between the submersible and non-submersible pumps as both work equally well. But make sure you pay attention to the quality and buy only high-quality pumps.

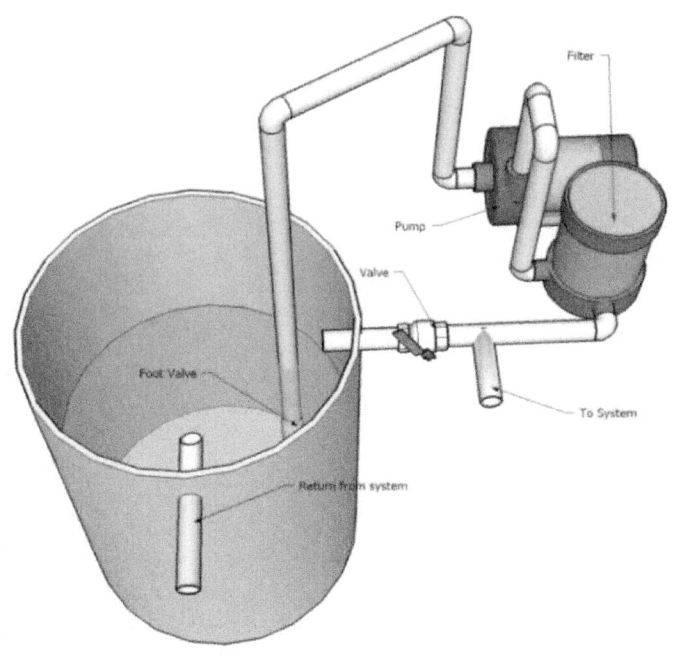

Tank

A tank or reservoir is needed to maintain the water and the nutrients that are drawn in by the systems. The water is drawn through pumps that supply it to the hydroponics system. Make sure you choose a tank that is made of a strong material and can hold the water and nutrients required to provide to your garden. The material should be high quality so that it is easier to maintain and does not easily turn dirty. Self-cleaning tanks are preferred and will help you maintain your garden for longer.

How to Assemble A DIY Hydroponic System Step-By-Step

Learning to grow food hydroponically is a great way to be more environmentally aware of your surroundings. You can grow more in less space. Also, it is absolutely great for small areas, especially when you just want a pinch of green in a tight space. You can grow flowers, herbs and other veggies that compliment your cooking. Let's get started with materials you will need for a water culture system.

Supplies

1. Opaque storage bin (it needs to hold water and come with a lid)
2. Mesh pots (how many is completely dependent upon what you're growing and the size of your container)
3. Chopped Rockwool grow cube (this is going to be your plant's growing medium)

4. Liquid growing solution (try Dyna-Grow brand; I have it and it yields great results every time)

5. Air pump (a small fish aquarium will suffice.)

6. Air stone and hose (again, from the fish isle at Wal-Mart is more than enough. You might need two stones based on how big your tank is)

Assembling Tools

1. Razor blade
2. Pencil (for marking)

Making Your System

In this step, I'm going to show you how to make a home for your precious pots and soon to be plants. It'll be really easy and fun to make too! Just be careful with that razor blade and use caution at all times!

Start by placing your pots upside down on the top of your storage bin. You're going to do this in order to make a home for your plant pots.

For this demonstration, I've use 6 mesh pots. Remember, how many you use will be completely dependent upon how big your container is, and how many plants you want to grill.

Take your pencil and trace around the top of the pot lip. Make sure that the lines do not overlap and give each pot its own place. This next step can be a bit tricky, but with pictures, I'm sure you will understand. Place the bottom base of your pot inside the larger hole you traced onto your lid. Make sure that it's centered.

Trace the smaller circle inside the larger circle traced around the pot lid. Cut away the small circle. From the outer circle to the hole you just make, make relief cuts. Look at the bottom picture below for clarification.

You want to put the relief cuts in so that your parts are held tightly and securely in the container lid. This will make a better seal for the aerated reservoir below.

Adding Aeration

This next step is important. I'm assuming that your container is clean and free of debris. If you just bought it, even better. However, you will need to sterilize it.

You don't want any bacteria in this container making your plant sick. Fill your container to the brim with water. Add 1 TBSP of bleach. No more.

You should keep your air stone in and start the pump so that the aeration mixes your sterilized solution. Put your pots in the container too. Let them soak for about 30 minutes. Afterwards, dump all the water and then allow to air dry ENTIRELY. Do this in order to get rid of the floor drain completely. Now you are ready to move into the first filling for your plant. It's time to start prepping your growing medium.

Initial Filling

You are almost done with your hydroponics water culture system. Follow the mixing directions on your nutrient solution container. With this particular system I will need 2 to 3 teaspoons per gallon because of how much water the container will have. Figure this amount out for your system and mix accordingly.

At the proper level, this container will be able to hold about 15 gallons of water. That means I need 15 teaspoons of the concentrated nutrient solution.

You can figure out your amount by starting with how many gallons of water will be in your container. Once you have done this, and measured out the amount of nutrients needed, you're ready to move on.

Start the aeration first, and then add the measured amount of nutrient solution. Before you do this make sure your garden is where you want it to be. It will be really heavy once you fill it up with water, and you will not be able to move it easily. Once you have your container filled, it's time to add your plants.

Adding Your Plants

For this guide I will actually be using plants that have already been started. I like to use herbs so that I can have them fresh for cooking.

Rockwool Note

Rockwool is derived from fiber glass. Precaution needs to be taken when working with this type of growing medium.

Use a dust mask, and as instructed, soak the medium in water for a while before handling.

Keeping the medium soaked with water will keep the fibers in each cube bound together, which will significantly reduce insulation risk. The inhalation risk of handling rock wool is no different than handling fiberglass insulation or accessing an attic that has been installed with fiberglass for insulation. Just be sure to wear a mask and use precaution.

Do not directly use your hands when touching Rockwool. Use a pot to scoop out the medium. It will shrink some, so take out more than what you think you'll need. You can estimate how much you need by measuring how much you plan to put into each pot.

Since I have six pots, I'm going to place the amount into a larger pot that will hold the entire amount of medium for my garden. Do the same for your own garden and then place into a larger container.

Fill with water and estimate how many gallons you added. You'll need to know about how many gallons of water you added so that you will be able to measure out the appropriate amount of nutrient solution for each pot. Now, soak the medium completely.

While your medium is soaking, wash off the dirt from your plant. Make sure there's no dirt remaining. Be very careful so that you do not damage the root system. Once the system has been completely cleared of dirt, put a bit of medium into the bottom of a pot. Put your plant in, and then pack the medium around your plant. Put the lid on your container and press the pot into the open hole. Repeat for the rest of your plants.

From Seeds

If you want to start from seed, you will need a few extra materials. The main thing is that you will need a Rockwool seed cube as well as a method to germinate. Essentially, you will soak the seed cubes, drop in a couple of seeds, and then place the seeds within your pots within the main medium. Make sure that you can see the top of your seed cube. NEVER put your seed into a dry cube as the fiber glass will likely damage the seed.

Keep your seed loved by watering with your hand. Make sure it gets enough water, but not too much. Also, you might want to place some type of cover or hood over the pot so that the conditions are better.

Maintenance

About every other week your water nutrient solution will need to be replaced. If you don't do this, the water will become toxic and the plant growth will be stunted. Your plants can even die. Larger reservoirs do not cause this type of toxicity because they have enough filtration coupled with the plant's ability to filter and remove toxins. When you are working in a small area, however, you will not have this.

While you are changing water, you will need to monitor the fluid levels. If the water gets too low, keep it topped off. When you start, keep the water level at the base of the pot. The root system will work its way out of the pot and into the container. Ultimately, it will get into the reservoir below.

When this happens, you will need to lower the water level, about an inch underneath your pots, and keep the aeration going. Aeration keeps your plant's root system from getting too wet; it will also help to be exposed to the air in between the pot and the reservoir.

Tips & Tricks

With this information, you can get started growing great plants. However, there are some extra things that you can do to really get your garden working well. I recommend a water level gauge. This is a clear hose that will connect to the bottom of your container and then run along the side of it vertically. This hose will show the water level. It will tell you when to top off, and it will also help you understand how much water your plants are using over time.

If you want to grow indoors, you'll need a grow light. Grow lights cost a considerable amount of money. If you can, you should definitely start your garden outdoors. However, this might not be an option for individuals in colder regions.

If you insert a valve to the bottom of your reservoir BEFORE you fill it up, draining will be really easy because you will be able to drain into a bucket and then use that water on other plants in the area.

You also want to monitor the pH levels of your water, as well as the conductivity. If you have a pool store in your area, they would likely offer free chemical testing for pH levels. You can also get pH level strips from some saltwater aquarium places too.

Pests & Diseases

Many gardeners like hydroponics for their garden because they find it easier for them to keep out pests and disease. Pests can destroy your harvest and eat through foliage. Plant disease can compromise the entire plant system.
Some people think that indoor hydroponic gardens can be free from pest issues. However, it can actually be easier for insects, plants, and disease to thrive on indoor systems. Some popular methods to combat pests and disease issues include:

Beneficial life forms

Certain types of fungi and bacteria keep pests at bay by crowding them out, consuming them, or creating compounds that are too toxic for them. This is a preferred method, as it is natural and considered organic. These organisms are considered beneficial because they keep away pests without harming the plant.

Insecticidal soaps are traditional and control pests, keeping disease away too. They have been used in all types of gardens for years, centuries even. The best soaps include naturally produced compounds, and non-toxic pest controls. They also do not leave behind harmful chemicals once the natural compounds are broken down from elemental exposure.

Neem oil is a favorite to use because it can deter more than 400 different pests found in soil-based plants and hydroponic garden. You use this oil by spraying the foliage, or leaves. Once the insects absorb the oil, the reproductive cycles are stopped, and the pests eventually die off. Be sure to do some more research on what pest control method would be best for you and your type of garden.

The Growing Medium

Whilst hydroponics means soilless way of growing plants, there are still media to be used in supporting the plants. In most systems, growers opt to use various types of "growing" medium that will support the roots of the plants and sustain the oxygen and water ratio. Getting the right medium is as important as acquiring the right hydroponic system.

In choosing the growing medium, consider the absorption it can provide and the support to keep the plants upright. The medium will greatly affect the amount of oxygen and nutrients your plants receive thus, it has a great impact on the plant's growth rates.

Things to consider

Before purchasing or setting the medium you will use, ask yourself first; will this medium be able to release adequate nutrients and oxygen? How well the medium can absorb the nutrients plays a huge, vital role in the plant's quality of yield and growth.

Likewise, you would want the growing medium to maintain oxygen which the plants need to grow. See to it that the medium can retain oxygen even when drench with water and nutrient solution. Moreover, the medium's capability to maintain water is important. There are mediums that are able to absorb water and keep it for longer.

Unfortunately, we cannot really say whether a medium is perfect or not. Various types of hydroponics systems can work better with some growing mediums compared to others. Hence, to determine the growing medium to use, consider first the type of hydroponic system you will use which is based on the plant you want to grow.

Certain plants would grow better and faster in a specific type of materials. Moreover, several types of systems work better in certain mediums. Below are some of the most common types of mediums you can use. Use this guide in determining the suitable medium for you.

8. **Rockwool**: is an extremely effective medium that has become popular for growers in recent years. It is primarily composed of melted limestone and granite. It is usually available in cubes that are perfect for beginners, but even commercialized and huge industrialized farms opt to use it.

This medium is efficient since it has an exceptional ability to hold oxygen and water. It offers the roots the incessant access to greater amount of oxygen and prevents dehydration of the plants. However, rock wool is known to be harmful to the skin and the lungs so be careful when using it. Its small fibers and dust can lodge into the lungs. To avoid this, immediately soak the rock wool in water after taking it out from its package.

Moreover, it is best to use with ebb-and flow, nutrients-film technique, drip and deep-water culture systems and in contrast with aquaponic system.

9. **Vermiculite**: this is a mined mineral. Vermiculite is subject to extreme heat making it expand before you can use it as a medium. It is normally used with another growing medium called as perlite as they complement each other very well. It has the ability to sustain moisture while perlite does the opposite. However, you cannot use the vermiculite solely as it tends to hold too much water thus, drowning the plants. A mixture of perlite and vermiculite (75-25) is ideal or an equal ratio of 50-50. Since this material is very lightweight, it is not advisable to use with the ebb-and-

flow system or it will be washed away. It is best to use in aeroponic and drip systems.

10. **Perlite**: is also a mineral and similar with vermiculite, it should be exposed to extreme heat before it can be used a medium. Likewise, it is one of the most inexpensive medium and has the ability to retain oxygen and nutrients longer. However, the biggest downside of it is that it easily loses moisture which is why growers opt to use it with vermiculite, coco coir and soil.

Moreover, this is not advisable to use with the ebb-and-flow system since it is very lightweight and porous that can be easily wash away during flooding. Likewise, this medium is ideal for growing long-term crops but make sure that there is no moisture deficiency which is the usual problem in using perlite.

11. **Grow Rocks**: essentially; these are clay pellets that were exposed to intense heat causing the clay to expand. The process leaves the clay with plenty of air pockets which makes it ideal in retaining oxygen. However, grow rocks cannot retain water efficiently. Growers use other moisture-retaining mediums and compounds in conjunction to grow rocks. Coconut fiber

is the most common partner of grow rocks and scientists even consider them the best possible combination of growing medium. The downside is that grow rocks are quite expensive, but they can be reused for a longer period and is ideal for ebb-andoflow and aquaponic systems.

12. **Coconut fiber / Coco coir**: shares the same popularity with rock wool. It has all the advantages of the rock wool but performs better in terms of oxygen and water retention. Moreover, it is completely organic (a by-product of coconut farming) compare to rock wool that is known to be health hazard. The coco coir is made from the coconut husk which makes it an ideal growing medium. The husk will protect the plants and is good for germination. Plus, it promotes great air to water ratio so the roots will not drown.

However, the market also sells lesser quality coconut fiber products so make sure that you are getting the good ones. A low-quality coconut fiber has excessive quantity of salt which can damage the plants. It is usually used with growing rocks and recommended for ebb and flow, drip and aquaponic systems.

13. **Air**: in most systems, the growing medium should be filled deeply so that the roots would be entirely submerged but in some systems such as the aeroponic system, the roots hang freely, enabling its access to nutrient solution. Air as a growing medium is recommended to use in deep water culture system and nutrient-film technique system.

14. **Oasis cubes**: they are similar to Rockwool, but more effective in terms of seedling and germination. It works similarly with the green foam-like material you usually see where flowers are embedded. Moreover, it is inexpensive and do not require pre-soaking. However, the downsides of oasis cubes are being inorganic and are only ideal for germination but not as growing medium for full-term plants.

15. **Starter plugs**: also known as the sponge start, starter plugs are the newest hydroponic media space introduced. The good thing about is that it's made from organic compost. Because of the biodegradable binding elements, it doesn't break apart. It is also ideal to use in growing seeds and clones before

introducing them to your hydroponic system. Starter plugs are relatively sustainable and is a good medium to grow large quantities of plants. The roots will grow straight downward making it easier for you to transplant them in the system. The downside is, it is expensive and is only ideal for cloning or starting seeds. They are also prone with fungus gnats which can affect the plants.

16. **Rice hulls**: are the shells of the rice grain. Like the coco fiber and coco coir, rice hulls are the by-products that would normally turn to waste so growers opt to re-purpose them by using them in their hydroponics system. However, this medium is not yet that popular since it can only hold little water and decays over time.

17. **Gravel**: this material is usually used in aquariums. Any type of it, as long as it's carefully washed can be used. Gravel is easier to clean, readily available and relatively cheap thus, it is a great starter medium for beginners. It also has the ability to drain well however, certain plant's roots may dry out especially the heavy types. When working with it, make sure that it will not get in contact with water as it may result to pH swings.

18. **Pumice**: is another lightweight mineral similar to perlite. It is capable of retaining high level of oxygen but does not work well with ebb and flow systems.
19. **Sand**: is the most abundant among these mediums and extremely cheap or for free. It is ideal for beginners but require frequent sterilization. Moreover, it is also heavy when wet and has poor water retention ability. Certain hydroponic systems are also not compatible with sand.
20. **Wood fiber**: is an efficient growing medium for hydroponics. Entirely organic, wood fiber is also said to reduce growth regulators which means, larger plants than the usual. The main downside of it is that it is prone to pests which can harm the plants.
21. **Polystyrene packing peanuts**: are the usual packing peanuts that are available everywhere. It is cheap and drains fairly well. Moreover, this is typically used in Nutrient Film Technique system but there is a greater possibility of contamination as the plants can absorb the styrene.
22. **Brick shards**: or crushed bricks work similarly with gravel. These do not have neutral pH so it may affect the water's pH level. And due to the brick dust, it requires frequent thorough cleaning.

Keep in mind that it is impossible to find out what is the best growing mediums as every type of hydroponics systems and plants require different characteristics and abilities. Hence, understanding each type of medium will help you decide wisely on what to use.

Starting Seeds

It is most satisfying when you plant a seed and nurture it until it becomes a full-grown plant and provides you with the intended harvest.

Of course, it takes more effort to grow a plant from seed than it does from a seedling, you need to decide if this is your preferred method and discover the best way of starting seeds.

Hydroponics is an excellent system for starting seeds as you have complete control over the elements your seeds are exposed to.

Seeds vs. Seedlings

For your first attempt at hydroponics, it is quicker to plant seedlings. However, controlling all the elements of the growing process includes controlling the seeds. If you decide to plant seeds, you will have complete control over the type and quality of the seed you plant.

Put simply, you can have any variety of seed but not necessarily any variety of seedling.

Seeds are generally easier to get hold of then seedlings.

The other consideration is the growing media. In hydroponics, you avoid using soil. However, unless you have a hydroponic center near you, the seedlings you purchase are likely to be grown in soil. This means carefully removing the soil to avoid contamination of your system. Unfortunately, washing them can damage the roots of the seedling.

Besides, seeds are cheaper than seedlings, allowing you more opportunities for failure without breaking the bank.

With proper planning and equipment, you are better off growing the plants from seed.

Starting Your Seeds

The best way to start seeds is to use a seed starter cube. A cube the size of one and a half inch will fit perfectly in a two-inch net pot. These small cubes are capable of holding water while air can reach the roots, which is the most important while germinating seeds.

First, you need to soak your grow cubes in chlorine or chloramine free water with a pH of 5.5. Water from your tap will be around 7-8 ph.

You most likely need to use a pH down solution.

Getting the chlorine out of your tap water is quite easy. Let it sit for one day for the chlorine to evaporate. If you want it to evaporate faster, you can use an air stone to air the chlorine out much quicker.

If your water company uses chloramine, you need a reverse osmosis filter to remove the chloramine. Note that not every reverse osmosis filter can remove chloramine. Chloramine can't be aired out and needs to be filtered. If you do not have a reverse osmosis filter available, you can use one thousand mg (one gram) of vitamin C (ascorbic acid) per forty gallons (one hundred and fifty liters) of water.

Use a tray to soak the cubes, pour the water on top, and let it sit for a few minutes. Once most of the water is absorbed, you need to drain the rest of the water. Do not squeeze the cubes. This will remove air pockets inside the cubes.

The next step is dropping your seeds into the holes. This can be a big task if you need to do a lot of seeds. Commercial growers use pelleted seeds and a vacuum seeder to speed this process up. Pelleted seed is a seed that is wrapped in clay. it is bigger, thus easier to handle.

You could also use a toothpick and dip the tip in some water. This will make the seed stick to the toothpick, as shown in the following image.

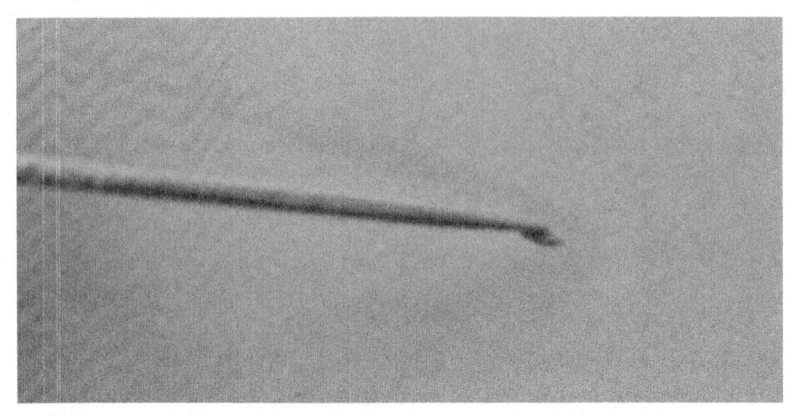

Using a wet toothpick to pick up seeds

If the holes of the grow media are preventing you from dropping the seed in, use a pen or a toothpick to open the hole back up.

You can use more than one seed per hole if the germination rate is bad. I always use two seeds per hole. When both seeds germinate, I keep the best one and use scissors to remove the bad one.

Placing the seed into the seed starter cube

Next, place your humidity dome on top of the tray to keep the seed starter cubes moist. Generally, the seeds don't need water until they have germinated. If you notice that your seed starter cubes are drying out, you can pour some more water in the tray. Don't forget to drain the rest of the water.

Rockwool cubes with seedling - Image from bootstrap farmer

Once the seeds start showing its first two leaves, you need to put it under a light source. This will provide the plant with the energy they need to grow. If you experience that the stems are growing long (stretching). It means that your plant is reaching for light. Increase the light on the seedlings to avoid this stretching. Do not use red light on seedlings. White fluorescents that are 6500K are perfect.

After ten days, you can transplant them to your system. If you are growing in a greenhouse, it can take fifteen days in winter.

Heat mats will increase germination during colder weather. The mats are placed under the seedling tray to warm up the seed starting cubes. Setting the heat mat to 68°F is recommended.

Recap:
1. Soak your seed starting cubes in chlorine or chloramine free water. Distilled water is even better. Make sure the pH is around 5.5.
2. Put the seed starting cubes in a tray.
3. Put the seed in the holes of the seed starter cubes.
4. Cover the seed starting cubes with a humidity dome.
5. Set the heat mat to 68°F (20°C) and place it under the tray.

6. Once sprouts appear, water them from the bottom with one quarter nutrient strength. The cubes will pick up the water.
7. Place them under T5 fluorescent lights. The humidity dome is still on the tray.
8. When you see four leaves and the roots are developing out of the seed starting cubes, it is time to transplant them to your growing system.

Nutrients during seeding

Seeds don't need nutrients initially as they are self-contained. However, you can give them a quarter-strength solution, compared to what you are using in your adult plant hydroponic system.

Germinating Seeds and Transplanting the Seedlings

The most initial step in your plant growth is seed germination.

The success of seed germination determines, to a great extent, the health and growth success of your plant. Thus, it is important to ensure that seed germination is given due preparation and desired attention.

When a seed begins to germinate, the roots begin to come out of the bottom of the seed and the shout starts to come out of the top of the seed. This makes the plant seedling, which will become the plant you are growing. Most of the time people germinate the seeds in the soil, but with hydroponics it is a bit different.

Always start the seeds in a dampened growing medium. It is best when the growing medium is damp, and not soaked. The depth to shoot for is about 1/8' inch depth. Some seeds are different for instance, Lettuce just barely needs to be covered and the same goes for Basil. It is best to research the specific seed and the right depth it needs.

In most cases, the seedlings will be ready to be transplanted in about two weeks. If this is being done indoors, they can be placed at a window that gets a good amount of light that comes through it throughout the day. A Fluorescent Grow Light can be used also. It is best to keep the fluorescent grow light a couple of inches above the seeds. The best temperature for this is around 70-80°F. You do not want them to be too hot or they will burn up.

A good root system is important before transplanting the seedlings. When the seeds are about 2-3 inches high you should start to see the roots coming out, then they are ready to be transplanted.

Types of Growing Mediums to Use When Germinating Seeds

Germinating with Rockwool

Germinating your seeds hydroponically can be done in various ways. One way is using Rockwool. There are Rockwool cubes that are made for germinating your seeds. The best sizes would be 1 inch or 1.5-inch cubes. If your Rockwool dries Out, you can lower the plant container in the water tray. If you are using a timer make sure it is working properly. Sometimes it can get off time. You can also check the hose to the water and see if it is connected properly.

Germinating with Perlite

You will need a tub or small container and fill it Perlite or Vermiculite. Perlite seems to be the better of the two because it does not mess with the PH Balance and creates air space.

You can place the seeds in rows or however, you would like as long as they have enough space from each other to grow. It is best to not go more than two inches deep when putting the seeds in the Perlite.

Starting the seedlings in root cubes

This is a great way to start multiple seeds at once. The root cubes are a tray that you place the seeds into. The tray is made of multiple cubes and you place a seed into the hole of each cube.

Starting the seedlings with plug trays

Plugs trays are different from root cubes, because you will need a growing medium. The plug trays come in different sizes; the most commonly used size is the #50 which means it has 50 plugs to start seeds into. You can use many different growing mediums.

Starting with dome and heat pad

These are starter kits that you can purchase. There is a plant tray with a dome top and underneath is a heating mat, also known as a propagation dome. They do come in different sizes. Instructions should come with the starter kit you purchase. Another option is to use tuber-ware with a lid and place a Hydroponic Heating Pad underneath.

Can you transplant plants from soil? The answer is yes. Just wash off the roots and get all the soil off first.

Process of Germinating the Seeds

Materials required
- Seeds
- Hydroponic cloner
- 2-inch net pot
- Starter plug (preferably Rapid Rooter)
- Air pump
- Air stone
- Tubing

Procedure

- Get your materials ready
- Fill your cloner with water – tap water can do well.
- Insert air stone into the reservoir and connect the tubing. Plug it in and switch on to test. Switch off after testing
- Soak the starter plugs into water. Once properly soaked, place it into the net pot.
- Insert seeds into a starter plug. For vegetables such as cabbage, eggplant, broccoli, tomatoes, basil, peppers, and cucumbers; plant 2-3 seeds per plug.
- Place the plugs in the nursery tray.
- Water daily by adding a seedling solution to the drain pan (not the cubes/plus).

Process of Transplanting the Seedlings

1. Preparing to transplant
2. Start hardening off your plant
3. Prepare the seedbed
4. Transplanting

Preparing to transplant

- Make sure that the hydroponic infrastructure is well set and working
- Make sure that the grow-on medium is properly set and ready
- Make sure that the following environmental conditions are appropriate:
  - Light control
  - Aeration control
  - Grow-on medium
  - Temperature control
  - pH level control
  - Nutrients

Hardening off

Survival mode enables them to easily adapt to a new environment with a minimal shock, if any. The following are some of the ways to harden off your seedlings;

- Prune excessive branches

- Gradually reduce the amount of light
- Gradually cut down on the amount of nutrient consumption
- Gradually increase or decrease the amount of water consumption so as to match the consumption expected of the new environment
- Gradually adjust the temperature to match that of the expected new environment
- Gradually adjust pH level to match that of the expected new environment

Preparing the Seedbed

- Immediately prior to transplanting, dig up holes within the growing medium wide and deep enough for the entire plug to be inserted.
- Have sufficient material to support the plant once transplanted

Transplanting

- Carefully take the hardened-off seedlings in their starter plugs from the tray and insert into the already dug holes in the seedbed (net pot).
- Support the transplanted seedlings with appropriate support material of the respective grow medium.
- Set the hydroponic system in motion (pump on, light on, etc.) so that the plants can start receiving nutrients and continue in their growth path.

How to Clone A Plant Using Hydroponics?

Cloning your plants

The cloning of plants is one of the easiest and fastest ways of multiplying your plants without worrying on gender. A clone is a small piece of plant that has been extracted or cut from the original mother plant.

Clones are usually pure copies of the original mother plant and usually contain the same genes and characteristics as the parent. If you notice that your plant is among the best in the market or maybe it's resilient to some pests or environmental conditions, you can simply clone them to produce multiple "copies". With that being said, we will focus on some effective techniques you can use to clone healthy and perfect plants.

How to clone a plant

The first step to take when cloning a plant is disinfecting all your tools such as scissors/razors and getting everything ready for the "operation". Look for strains that show pure signs of maturity and good health before cutting preferably new strains. To detect mature strains, always check on the leaves/node's connection (the leaves/nodes should be alternating and shouldn't be connected at the same exact point on the stem).

When cutting, choose a spot where there's a fresh growing stem and cut at an angle of 45°. Ensure that the new cutting is about 5-8 inches for more desirable results.

Some people may choose to split the bottom of their cutting or scrap it a bit to expose more of the inside. This idea is perfect as it promotes faster rooting.

After you've cut your clone, trim the lower leaves and soak it in water so it can develop roots by itself. In case the leaves are not trimmed, you clone may focus more on making leaves grow instead of focusing on developing roots. Some growers prefer to induce rooting hormones for faster root growth. This can be done through dipping the freshly cut stems into a gel or rooting hormone powder.

Roots developing on a clone

Now that you have the clones ready, a wise grower will place them inside a humidity dome, a heating pad or an automatic cloner. Usually, new clones require weak light and warm temperatures to develop roots faster. Therefore, you should expose them to temperatures ranging from 72-77°F (22-25°C) and an 18/6 night/dark cycle for the first 10 days. Depending with the parent plant, clones may take 7 days to 2 weeks to fully develop a strong rooting system. Always be patient and wait until the roots are fully formed to transplant your plants.

The Best Plants to Choose for Hydroponics

With hydroponic gardening, you can grow almost anything from houseplants and flowering plants to vegetables and fruits. Whether you are growing them for decoration, health purposes or for seasoning, you will find hydroponic gardening quite beneficial. You can grow your own plants in any season and weather and have your own supply of fresh herbs, fruits, and vegetables.

Here is a list of the plants that will grow well in various hydroponic systems. Also included is some interesting information about each of them.

Herbs

You will be happy to know that many herbs grow exceedingly well in hydroponic systems. Some of them include basil, anise, chamomile, chives, catnip, cilantro, chervil, dill, fennel, mint, lavender, oregano, marjoram, parsley, sage, rosemary, thyme and tarragon.

Basil – Basil if often grown in a protected environment so it thrives in a hydroponic system. Trim and harvest it weekly once it is mature. You can enjoy basil with many dishes and salads.

Anise – Anise seeds and leaves provide a licorice taste. This can be useful in salads, flavor confections and as a garnish. Anise plants grow rapidly from the seed to about 1-2 feet in height. A month after the anise blooms, the seeds can be gathered, used and re-planted.

Chamomile – Everyone loves chamomile tea as it not only tastes good but also has medicinal properties. This herb grows suitably in a soilless culture and takes only 6 – 12 weeks before you can fully enjoy the benefits.

Chives – These herbs require minimal space to grow and tolerate various kinds of growing conditions so they will easily adapt in a hydroponic system. You will enjoy chives as seasoning for main dishes and salads, as they are very aromatic.

Catnip – This herb grows well whether in partial shade or full sun. A perennial that can grow up to 3-5 feet in height, it will flourish well in a hydroponic system. You can propagate the catnip through seed, root ball or stem cutting.

Cilantro – The cilantro will endure various conditions of pH and light; needs very little maintenance and you can harvest it in 6 weeks. It is a perfect herb to grow hydroponically. Once mature, trim regularly.

Chervil – You have to remember that chervils require low lighting and cool temperatures. You need to set up your hydroponics system where there is shade and special cooling. You can harvest chervils in just 4 weeks. It is best to grow this herb during winter.

Dill – Dill is a flavorful hydroponic herb that produces new growth every time you harvest it. You can make numerous cuttings from the lush growth of the compact leaf. It is best to replace the spent plants every 3-4 weeks, so you have a continuous supply of dill.

Fennel – Fennel looks like dill, with finely divided leaves. This herb may grow from seed to about 3-4 feet in height. Fennel seeds are as condiments and you can harvest them when ripened. You can eat the flower stalks and leaves in salads.

Mint – Mint is mostly aquatic or semi-aquatic making hydroponic systems the perfect medium for growing the different varieties. Peppermint, orange mint, and spearmint are some the mints that flourish in soilless culture.

Lavender – The lavender is a fragrant herb that is also a decorative plant. Lavender is used to make oil, vinegar and lavender water and as a perfume for linens and clothing. It can grow well in hydroponic environments.

Oregano – You can use Oregano leaves whether they are fresh or dried. They have medicinal properties and you can use them as a flavoring for pizza, Italian sauces and meat such as lamb.

You can stimulate its foliage when you cut back the flowers, but you need to replant them as soon as they become woody.

Marjoram – Marjoram is another fragrant herb for flavoring for meat dishes and dressings. This herb can be sown in flats or plugs. Then they are transplanted in hydroponic units. You can harvest 6 – 10 weeks after planting the seeds.

Parsley – Parsley is well suited for hydroponic systems because of its long taproot. Make sure that your container is at least a foot deep so you can get the best growing result for this delicious herb.

Sage – You can add sage to sausages and dressings. You can grow sage in a hydroponic environment, provided that the herbs get enough sunlight and are protected from the cold. Harvest sage leaves before they bloom and dry them in well-ventilated rooms, away from sunlight.

Rosemary – The aromatic leaves of rosemary are used as seasoning and can be manufactured to produce medicinal oil. The herb needs protection from cold temperatures and will thrive when placed under full sunlight.

Thyme – This herb will grow well in almost any conditions. It requires very minimal fertilization and will flourish in hydroponic systems, especially when it is planted in the early spring.

Tarragon – While it is not aromatic until the tops and leaves harvested, the tarragon is essential for seasonings. It has a sweet smell and the oils are quite fragrant.

Vegetables

Grow your own vegetables at home and enjoy the fact that they are organic and insecticide free. Some of the vegetables that thrive in a hydroponic garden are the following: lettuce, artichokes, spinach, beans, cabbage, asparagus, beets, broccoli, Brussels sprouts, cauliflower, and peas. Leafy greens grow very well hydroponically and require less maintenance.

You can also grow watercress indoors, making hydroponic systems a perfect choice to cultivate this low-growing perennial. Be sure to harvest it before the flower buds appear so it remains edible.

The following vegetables usually grow in soil, but you can cultivate them hydroponically:

23. Onions
24. Carrots
25. Potatoes
26. Leeks
27. Parsnips
28. Radishes
29. Yams

Think carefully before you start planting any of these vegetables because they require extra care. If you have the time and can exert the effort, you will enjoy growing them.

Here are some veggie crops to avoid:

30. Zucchini
31. Summer squash
32. Corn
33. Plants that vine

While they can be grown hydroponically, it will not be very practical when it comes to space. These crops can easily take too much space. Hydroponic garden systems should be compact.

Fruits

Hydroponic gardening lets you grow fruits all year-round. Water-loving fruits such as grape, cantaloupe, tomatoes, blueberries, strawberries and raspberries can be grown in a hydroponics system. Some farmers can even grow pineapples with this gardening system.

Flowers

Hydroponic gardening will allow you to grow flowers in large numbers. Most flowers do well in a hydroponic culture. The challenge is that every plant has particular needs – this means that they cannot be mixed in one hydroponic unit. For example, roses need larger amounts of potassium compared to daisies. Some plants can grow simultaneously in one unit. You need to be knowledgeable and very careful in matching flower species, so they get the right nutrient mix.

Succulents are not a good choice for hydroponic gardening, as they grow better in dry conditions.

Nutrient Solutions

If you are a beginner with hydroponics, you may choose to just purchase a nutrient solution. This saves you some time and since there are so many good ones to choose, it helps you to get through the process, at least for the first year, without having to worry about having the right nutrients or other issues.

When you look at the solution, you will notice that there are percentages for NP-K on the package.

These are important nutrients and you should make sure that they make up the majority of the solution.

The higher concentration they are, the better this solution is for your plants. The rest of the solution is often going to be filler, although the good brands will have other micronutrients that are good for your plants.

This is not an area to skimp on when it comes to your hydroponic garden. While you may be interested in saving some money along the way, this is the main source of nutrients that your plants will get. They will not find nutrients from the soil or other locations, so you are responsible for getting the right solution to help out. Look for the best one you can find that has a lot of healthy nutrients and your plants are going to grow better than ever before.

After going through this process a few times, you may feel that it is time to take on the challenge and create some of your own solutions in the process. This is a bit trickier, but it does ensure that you are giving your plants the very best when it comes to their nutrition. You can choose to do this as a beginner, but remember it is a bit trickier and you will have to find all the ingredients on your own. If you are interested in doing this process, here are some easy formulas that can make your crops grow like crazy.

Vegetable Crops

34. 6 grams of Calcium Nitrate
35. 46 grams of Sulfate of Potash
36. 2.09 grams of Potassium Nitrate
37. 1.39 grams of Monopotassium Phosphate
38. .4 grams of 7 percent Fe Chelated Trace Elements
39. 2.42 grams of Magnesium Sulfate

Fruit Crops

40. 8 grams Calcium Nitrate
41. 1.70 grams Sulfate of Potash
42. 2.80 grams of Potassium Nitrate
43. 1.30 grams of Monopotassium Phosphate
44. 40 grams trace elements
45. 2/4 grams of Magnesium Sulfate

Flowering Crops

46. 46 grams Potassium Nitrate
47. 4.10 grams Calcium Nitrate
48. 1.39 grams Monopotassium Phosphate
49. 1.39 grams Sulfate of Potash
50. .40 grams trace elements
51. 2.40 grams Magnesium Sulfate

When doing this process, consider dissolving each element one at a time. This ensures that the element is going to have the chance to dissolve completely for use. All of the formulas will need a gallon of water, so fill up a container with this amount, making the water warm, and then add each salt one at a time for the best results.

The trace elements are just as important as the rest, but you can usually get a mixture that has them all together. Make sure that you have some iron, manganese, zinc, copper, boron, and Molybdenum in the mixture to ensure that it is going to keep those plants looking nice and strong for a long time to come.

PH Importance

Another thing that you will have to watch out for when it comes to your plants is their PH level. If these numbers are too low, you could have some issues with the plants being able to flower the way that you want. On the other hand, if you have the pH too acidic, it is going to kill off the plant in the process. You may want to consider having a meter that will watch for the concentration of salts in the solution so that the pH stays pretty much the same. If the pH gets a little off, the plants are not going to grow as much as you would like.

For most plants, you will want to keep the pH around 6.0 to 6.5; going too much below or above this amount is going to make it bad for the plants. Find a good kit that you can use to check the pH on occasion to ensure that you are giving the plants the very best environment for them to grow in.

PH is the potential hydrogen-hydroxyl ion content. To make it easier, let's think about a scale where you are weighing two items. One side you have some acidic juice and on the other, you have some bread or your base. Much like the scale, when we use the pH in hydroponics it's important that the scale is weighed equally by both.

Often overlooked, understanding and checking the pH level has a huge impact on the product you will grow.

Water has an equal balance of both hydrogen and hydroxyl and therefore has a neutral pH level of 7. Each level of pH in a solution multiplies as it increases. If the pH level in your solution is 4.0 then it contains ten times more acid than something where the pH level is 3.0 and so on. Based on your plants, what this means is if your pH level needs to be 6.0 to 7.0 you would have to adjust the pH level ten times more than the current level. I know it sounds complicated, but trust me, it's something that is good to know if you want to create a wonderful hydroponic system. Each type of plant will need a different pH level and it's nice to have a reference for it. Here are some of the common plant pH levels you may need to know in the future:

52. Cabbage 6.5-7.5
53. Cucumbers 5.9-6.1
54. Lettuce 6.0-6.5
55. Pumpkin 5.1-6.6
56. Radish 6.0-7.0
57. Strawberries 5.5-6.5
58. Tomatoes 5.5-6.5

When you need to check or adjust your pH it is fairly simple and there are several ways to do so. Typically, the best way to check your pH level is to purchase paper test strips, which have a dye and allow you to compare the color of your water with the levels they show you. The only issues with this are that often the color differences can be hard to distinguish between. Another way to check your pH levels would be to purchase a liquid pH test kit. With this test, you add a slight amount of dye to a water sample. Similar to using the test strips, this way is more accurate to read and often gives better results. Lastly, if you're a hardcore gardener, you can purchase a digital pH meter. Obviously the most accurate, they can come in big pieces of equipment or in something as small as a pen. Either way, you use an electrode to test the sample water and are given the results. Find the right supplies for what you're doing and be sure to have some on hand whenever you need to test the pH levels in your hydroponic garden.

So now you've checked the pH level but how do you adjust it? The easiest and most effective things to have on hand are phosphoric acid (to decrease your pH) and potassium hydroxide, (to increase your pH). These are relatively harmless things you can easily buy and keep on hand.

If you're not comfortable using them, you can buy pH adjusters at local stores where everything has been mixed and is ready to go. The only issues with these are that they often cause huge shifts in the pH level and are harder to control. Adjust the pH level in your system slowly and be sure to check it regularly, and more often, after a change has been made to be sure the pH level is doing what you want it to. Over time you will develop a system that works for you and will have no issues adjusting the pH level next time. Don't be alarmed if the pH levels go up over time this is normal just be sure to check it with some regularity.

Different Kind of Nutrients

This Chapter will discuss the different types of Nutrients you can use for your Hydroponic Plants.

You can either use ready mix nutrient solutions or mix the nutrients yourself. It is up to you and what you would prefer to do. Sometimes it can be easier to use the ready mix. You just have to make sure to select the right one for the plants you are going to grow and use the right proportions to the amount of water being used.

In this section I will discuss both the ready mix and the do it yourself mix. As mentioned, each plant or vegetable will probably have different nutrient requirements.

NPK Ratio

One thing you will need to get familiar with while dealing with Plant Nutrients is the NPK Ratio. NPK stands for Nitrogen, Phosphorus, and Potassium which are the chemicals that make up the fertilizer. This ratio is shown on most fertilizer bags as a series of three numbers which would look like for example 20-20-20. The numbers indicate the contents of each of the three chemicals. It is important to know what the ratio is for the plants you are trying to grow. If this ratio is off it can kill the plant. These nutrients are normally found in the soil, but sometimes the soil does not contain the right amounts, so people add them with fertilizers. In the case of hydroponic plants there is no soil, so these nutrients will need to be added.

Macronutrients and Micronutrients

It is also a good idea to be familiar with the Macronutrients and Micronutrients needed for plants to grow. This does not really change from plants grown in soil or hydroponically.

Macronutrients: These nutrients are broken into two different categories. The categories are primary and secondary. The primary macronutrients are what the plant uses to grow, and these are Nitrogen, Phosphorus, and Potassium. These are the nutrients used for the NPK Ratio when selecting your nutrient solution. The secondary macronutrients are Sulfur, Calcium, and Magnesium. Normally plants produce the secondary macronutrients themselves when grown in the ground. Since, hydroponic plants do not contain soil these macronutrients can be added to the water in the nutrient tank.

Micronutrients: Sometimes micronutrients are called "Trace Elements." These are nutrients that are also needed to make your plants grow and are to be in small amounts. That is why they are call "micro" nutrients. The micronutrients in plants are Molybdenum, Zinc, Iron, Chloride, Boron, Manganese, and Copper.

What are the Different Types of Solutions to Use? There are many different kinds of Nutrient Solutions Hydroponic Growers use. There are one-two and three-part mixes, Super Shot, Bloom Mix, and a lot more. A lot of Hydroponic Growers like to make their own Nutrient Solution. Some Hydroponic Growers like to use a Pre-Made Nutrient Formula. This can seem to be very confusing on which one is the right one to use. It really is up to you which type you prefer.

Some Pre-Made Nutrient Solutions:

59. **Hoagland Solution**: This Nutrient Solution has been around since the 1950's. It contains a lot of Nitrogen and Potassium. It is great for big fruit plants like peppers and also tomatoes.

60. **Steiner Solution**: This Nutrient Solution provides micronutrients for Flowering Plants and Foliage instead of Fruit Plants

How often do you need to change the Nutrient Solution? It is best to change the Nutrient Solution every 2 to 3 weeks.

Different Plant Nutrient Needs: Some plants required more Nutrients than others. The plants that require more nutrients are called "Heavy Feeders" and the plants that require fewer nutrients are called "Light Feeders." Below is a chart showing some plants that are Heavy Feeders and plants that are Light Feeders.

Heavy Feeders		Light Feeders	
Asparagus	Lettuce	Carrot	Alfalfa
Beet	Okra	Garlic	Beans
Broccoli*	Parsley	Leek	Clover
Brussels sprouts*	Pepper	Mustard Greens	Peas
Cabbage*	Potato	Onion	Peanut
Cantaloupe*	Pumpkin*	Parsnip	Soybeans
Cauliflower	Radish	Rutabaga	
Celery	Rhubarb	Shallot	

Collard	Spinach	Sweet Potato	
Corn, Sweet*	Squash, Summer*	Swiss Chard	
Eggplant*	Strawberry		
Endive	Sunflower		
Kale	Tomato*		
Kohlrabi	Watermelon*		

Pest and Disease Control

Crop health

One of the most significant issues with hydroponic crops, or any crop, is the risk of disease or pests. Either of these can quickly destroy your hard work and leave you without a crop. That's why it is so important to know how to deal with these issues.

Diseases

There are several ways in which disease can occur or be introduced to your plants. It is essential to be aware of what these are to prevent them from becoming an issue when you are growing your crops.

Root disease

You won't be surprised to learn that root disease affects the roots of your crops. It is generally caused by a lack of oxygen getting to the plant's root, effectively making them rot. In a hydroponics system, your roots may be in the water all the time, increasing the risk of root disease.

However, providing you maintain the levels of dissolved oxygen and keep the water moving, you shouldn't have an issue with root disease.

Wash your hands

Consider for a minute the number of different items you touch daily and you will quickly get an idea of the amount of dirt and contamination that you can carry unseen, on your hands.

This dirt, or bacteria, can be harmful to your plants, introducing bacteria that they don't know how to defend against. To prevent this from being an issue, you must always wash your hands or sanitize them before you enter your growing space and handle the plants or the system. Shoes and clothes are equally important.

Sanitize grow materials

A three percent bleach solution or a three percent hydrogen peroxide solution is the best way to keep the growing environment clean. Wipe every piece of equipment and surface with the solution after every harvest. This will prevent bacteria from getting to your plants and potentially killing them.

Keeping the area clean doesn't need to be difficult or time-consuming; it just needs to be consistent.

No organic material

Hydroponic systems don't use soil, which is good as soil carries hundreds of different bacteria. Many of which can be harmful to your plants.

However, just because you don't use soil doesn't mean that soil contamination can't happen. You will need to consider where your seedlings came from. If they were initially grown in soil, they are going to need to be cleaned thoroughly before being planted in the growing media.

Keeping all soil and plant material away from your hydroponic system will help to protect your plants. It is better to grow from seed instead of buying a seedling from the gardening store.

Possible Pests

Here is a list of possible pests. Afterward, I will give some tips on how to get rid of them organically.

Aphids

These tiny black or sometimes green dots can quickly suck the goodness out of any plant. They walk along the stems and suck the sap from the plant. This removes the nutrients and will make your plant ill; eventually, it will die.

Some of the most commonly mentioned aphids are greenfly and blackfly. They can breed incredibly quickly. It is important to treat them as soon as you find them; you don't want these pests spreading over to the rest of your crops.

An aphid (can be green or black)

Caterpillars

You already know what a caterpillar is. On its way to becoming a beautiful butterfly, it will chew through every green leaf it can find.

On the plus side, these pests are relatively easy to pick off and remove; check the underside of your leaves where they usually hide.

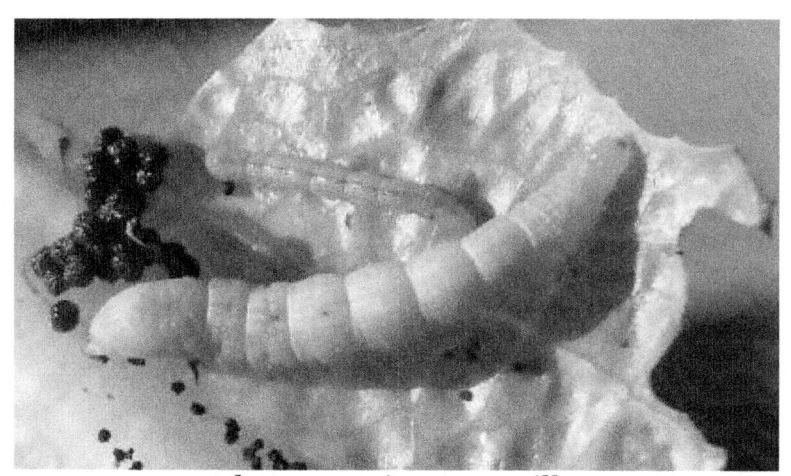

A lettuce eating caterpillar

Squash Bugs

Unsurprisingly, these bugs are most commonly found on squash plants. They may not be an issue to you if you are not growing any squash.

They look very similar to the stink bug, are approximately half an inch long, and have flat backs. The squash bug is gray and brown with orange stripes on the bottom of their abdomen.

You'll usually find them on the underside of your leaves in a group. They can fly but generally prefer to walk on your plants. These bugs will destroy the flow of nutrients to your plants.

A squash bug (picture courtesy of Donna Brunet)

Mealybugs

This is yet another pest that multiplies quickly once they find a home. They tend to prefer warmer environments. Your hydroponics setup will probably be ideal for growth! The amount of damage they do will depend on the number of pests you have; early detection is crucial.

Mealybugs are oval insects approximately a quarter inch long and covered with a white or gray wax.

A mealybug

Cutworms

The cutworm is the larvae of several different species of adult moths. They will generally hibernate for the winter months; unless your hydroponic system is warm enough to discourage this.

Once they finish hibernating, they will emerge and start eating the leaves of your plants. They generally feed at dusk; this is the best time to see them in action. They are effectively caterpillars but are often considered grubs. The exact size and look will depend on the species.

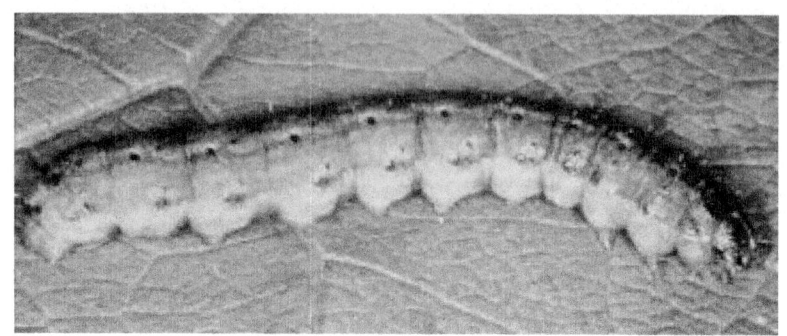

A black cutworm

Hornworms

You are most at risk of getting them if you have tomatoes. They are green, generally fat, and look like caterpillars.

The adult moth lays eggs on the underside of your leaves in the late spring. These will hatch in less than a week. You will then have larvae, which will start to eat your plants for the next four to six weeks until nothing is left but the stems.

A hornworm

They will generally go into a cocoon for the winter, but if your system is warm enough, they may only do this for a couple of weeks. They can then transform into moths and lay more eggs to feed on your plants.

What might surprise you is the size of the hornworm; it can be as much as five inches long! They are pale green and have white and black markings. They also have a horn at their rear, although this looks dangerous, they are not capable of stinging you.

You will find dark green droppings on the top of your leaves; this will tell you the hornworm is present; turn your leaf over to see them.

Dealing with Pests

Having a greenhouse where soil-based plants are located is a bad idea. Pests could use the soil as a breeding ground before they move on to your hydroponics setup.
Growing your produce from seed will drastically eliminate the possible pests that are on a plant. The plants you buy from your local dealer could be filled with pests already.

Sap Suckers

One of the best natural remedies for sapsuckers is to spray your plants with chili or garlic spray. However, these can affect the taste of your crop and in large quantities, can make it uncomfortable for the plants.
Moderation is the key. Alternatively, you can use beneficial insects.

Caterpillars

The simplest way of getting rid of caterpillars is to spray a substance called Bacillus thuringiensis. You should be able to get this in your local garden store.
It is a natural soil-borne bacterium that kills caterpillars and their larvae.

Mold & Fungus

Potassium bicarbonate is excellent at destroying virtually all molds and fungus. You can spray it directly onto any affected plants and the ones next to them.

Beneficial Insects

Another great way of dealing with pests in your system is to use beneficial insects. As the name suggests, these are insects that will help your system by eating the pests that do damage. It is a good idea to have them in your system year-round.

That means when there will be an outbreak, they might be able to limit it or negate the outbreak.

Although it might not be easy to introduce them to your outdoor system, it is preferably done indoors or in a greenhouse where they are contained.

Some of the best ones to consider are:

Ladybugs

These are great at getting rid of aphids before they can do any real damage. One ladybug can consume as many as five thousand aphids per year!

A ladybug

Parasitic Wasp

This tiny wasp doesn't sting. It will lay its eggs in the body of an aphid. The baby wasp eats the inside of the aphid before emerging to repeat the process.

The Parasitic Wasp

Praying Mantis

These slightly strange looking creatures are excellent at eating aphids, caterpillars, potato beetles, leafhoppers, hornworms, squash bugs, and pretty much any pest that could be a problem for your setup.

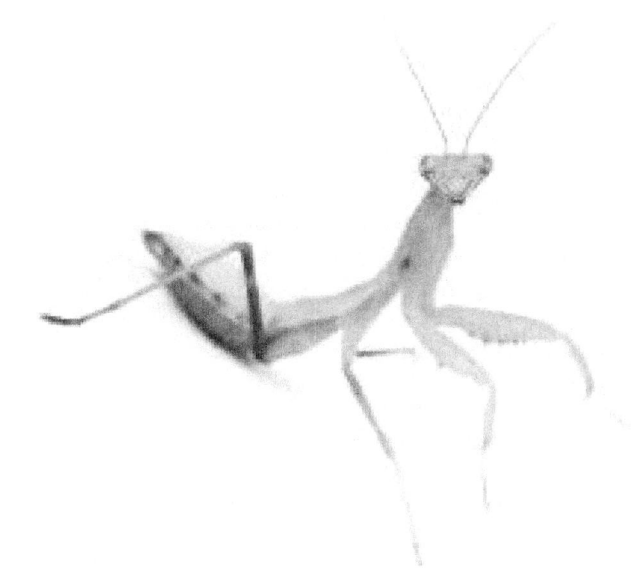

A praying mantis

Lacewings

These are good at attacking virtually all types of pests. You will find they are very good at eating aphids, mealybugs, whitefly, and even thrips. They can eat as many as one hundred aphids per week. They also work best at night when most of the pests are active.

It is worth noting that if you had a one thousand square foot greenhouse, you would need approximately two thousand lacewings. You can get these from most biological insect vendors, or you can try planting flowers that attract lacewings near your system.

A lacewing

Good flowers to plant are fennel, dill, coriander, dandelion, and angelica. They also like brightly lit windows.

Spider Mite Predators

The tiny spider mite can suck the nutrients out of two hundred different plants. Fortunately, you can solve the issue by introducing the bright orange spider mite predator. They may only live for roughly forty-five days, but they can consume as many as twenty spider mites each day!

Aphid Predator Midge

These tiny little bugs look like small mosquitoes. They can sniff out aphid colonies, and then they lay their eggs next to them.
Within a few days, the larva will hatch and eat the aphids. The aphid predator midge can consume as many as fifteen aphids a day.

A Midge

Nematodes

These are natural parasites that are so small you can only see them with a microscope. They can kill approximately two hundred and fifty different types of larvae.
Familiarize yourself with the most common pests in your area. Then you will know how to deal with them.

How To Fix The Most Common Nutrition Problems

Significant elements

Ammonium (NH4)

Poisonousness symptoms: plants provided with ammonium nitrogen (NH4–N) may display ammonium poisonous quality manifestations with sugar consumption and decreased plant growth; injuries may show up on plant stems, alongside descending measuring of leaves; rot of the conductive tissues at the bases of the stems and wilting under dampness stress; bloom end fruit decay will happen, and Mg lack side effects may likewise show up.

Calcium (Ca)

Deficiency symptoms: growing tips of roots and leaves will turn dark colored and die; the edges of leaves will look battered for the sides of developing leaves will stay together; fruit quality will be influenced, and bloom end spoil will show up on fruits.

Extra symptoms: plant leaves may show common Mg inadequacy manifestations; in instances of incredible overabundance, K insufficiency may likewise happen.

Magnesium (Mg)

Deficiency symptoms: older leaves will be yellow, with interveinal chlorosis (yellowing between veins) indications; growth will be moderate, and a few plants might be effectively plagued by ailment.

Extra symptoms: result is cation awkwardness with conceivable Ca or K inadequacy side effects showing up.

Nitrogen (N)

Deficiency symptoms: light green leaf and plant shading; more seasoned leaves turn yellow and will, in the long run, turn dark colored and die; plant growth is moderate; plants will develop early and be hindered.

Extra symptoms: plants will be dim green; new growth will be succulent; vulnerable if exposed to ailment, insect invasion, and dry season pressure; plants will effectively hold up; bloom fetus removal and absence of fruit set will happen.

Phosphorus (P)

Deficiency symptoms: plant growth will be moderate and hindered; more established leaves will have a purple hue, especially on the undersides.

Extra symptoms: excess side effects will be visual indications of Zn, Fe, or Mn lack; high plant P substance may meddle with ordinary Ca nourishment and run of the mill Ca inadequacy manifestations may show up.

Potassium (K)

Deficiency symptoms: edges of more established leaves will seem consumed, a side effect known as sear; plants will effortlessly hold up and be delicate to illness invasion; fruit and seed production will be debilitated and of low quality.
Extra symptoms: plant leaves will show common Mg and potentially Ca insufficiency indications because of cation lopsidedness.

Sulfur (S)

Deficiency symptoms: overall light green shade of the whole plant; more seasoned leaves turn light green to yellow as the inadequacy intensifies.
Extra symptoms: premature senescence of leaves may happen.

Micronutrients

Boron (B)

Deficiency symptoms: abnormal improvement of growing focuses (meristem tic tissue); apical growing focuses in the long run become hindered and die; flowers and fruits will prematurely end; for some grain and fruit crops, yield and quality are significantly diminished; plant stems might be weak and effectively break.
Extra symptoms: leaf tips and edges turn darker and die off.

Chlorine (Cl)

Deficiency symptoms: younger leaves will be chlorotic, and plants will effortlessly shrink.
Overabundance symptoms premature yellowing of the lower leaves with consuming of leaf edges and tips; leaf abscission will happen, and plants will effortlessly shrivel.

Copper (Cu)

Deficiency symptoms: plant growth will be moderate; plants will be hindered; young leaves will be misshaped, and growing focuses will pass on.

Extra symptoms: iron insufficiency may be induced with moderate growth; roots might be hindered.

Iron (Fe)

Deficiency symptoms: interveinal chlorosis on rising and young leaves with the possible death of the new growth; when extreme, the whole plant may turn light green.

Extra symptoms: Bronzing of leaves with minor darker spots, a common side effect on certain crops.

Manganese (Mn)

Deficiency symptoms: interveinal chlorosis of young leaves while the leaves and plants remain commonly green; when severe, the plants will be hindered.

Extra symptoms: older leaves will show dark-colored spots encompassed by chlorotic zones and circles.

Molybdenum (Mo)

Deficiency symptoms: symptoms are like those of N inadequacy; more seasoned and center leaves become chlorotic first, and, on certain occasions, leaf edges are rolled, and growth and blossom development are limited.
Overabundance symptoms: not known and presumably not of a normal event.

Zinc (Zn)

Deficiency symptoms: upper leaves will show interveinal chlorosis with brightening of influenced leaves; leaves might be little and misshaped, framing rosettes.
Extra symptoms: iron insufficiency manifestations will occur.

The Nutrient Solution

Likely no part of hydroponic growing is as misjudged as the detailing and utilization of nutrient solutions. Most messages just give the reader a rundown of nutrient solution equations, favored reagent sources, and the fundamental loads and measures to set up an aliquot of solution. Albeit such information is fundamental to set up a nutrient solution appropriately, an adequately based understanding of its administration is as significant, if not more, along these lines, for effective growth, numerous formulators and most growers do not comprehend the mind-boggling interrelationships among creation and use, and it is this part of the nutrient solution the executives for which a great part of the writing lamentably gives next to zero assistance. In an article about another growing machine for lettuce and herb production, called the "omega garden machine," the engineers of the machine expressed that the hardest part is getting the plant food right and realizing the amount to encourage.

Poor yields, scraggly plants, high water, and reagent costs, the greater part of the signs of a not exactly completely effective growing activity can be legitimately connected to defective definitions joined with the fumble of the nutrient solution. There are, shockingly, no total pat remedies or plans that can be given to growers by any hydroponic counselor. Growers should explore different avenues regarding their very own systems, watching, testing, and altering until the best possible harmony among arrangement and use is accomplished for their specific circumstance and specific plant species. However, it is amazing that, for some occasions, plants appear to have the option to modify, growing sensibly well, yet not at their genetic potential. Genetic potential plant production requires the exact administration of the nutrient component condition of the rooting medium.

Although much isn't thought about how best to detail and deal with a nutrient solution, there are numerous acceptable signs regarding what ought to or ought not to be finished. Growers utilizing these pieces of information should build up a plan of the executives that best accommodates their environmental hydroponic system and plant growing conditions, experimenting with different procedures to get the most extreme usage of the nutrient solution while accomplishing high crop yields of top quality.

The utilization of a specific nutrient solution detailing depends on three variables:

61. Hydroponic growing system.
62. Recurrence and pace of nutrient solution dosing of plant roots.
63. Plant nutrient component prerequisites.

The Fight Against Plant Diseases

Diseases constitute one of the limiting elements within the production of any crop. Hence, its control is a factor to keep in mind from sowing or transplantation to harvest.

Producing plants in hydroponic cultivation can reduce the incidence of many diseases that are associated with the soil. This is the case of seedling fall produced by a complex of natural soil-borne fungi (Pythium, Rhizoctonia, Botrytis, Fusarium, among others) radical rot caused by fungi of the genus Phytophthora and conductive vessel necrosis, associated with Fusarium species and verticillium. In this way, using this mode of production can be an alternative control of these pathologies. However, it is crucial to make sure that the irrigation water or the substrate used is not contaminated since, in the opposite case, the severity and incidence of the disease can be much greater than what would occur in a traditional soil crop. In hydroponic crops, fungi that affect the radical system can have a very rapid development in the absence of natural enemies.

Similarly, the high humidity conditions in this type of production, especially if it is carried out under a greenhouse, can be conducive to the infection, development, and dissemination of many phytopathogenic organisms such as fungi, bacteria, and viruses.

Together with the pathologies caused by living or biotic agents, there are also diseases that are caused by abiotic agents, which are called disorders. These in a hydroponic or soilless crop may be due to:

- phytotoxicity due to poor application of pesticides or other agrochemicals
- poor irrigation management
- Excess salts

- Lack or excess of certain nutrients
- Inadequate temperature
- Inappropriate pH

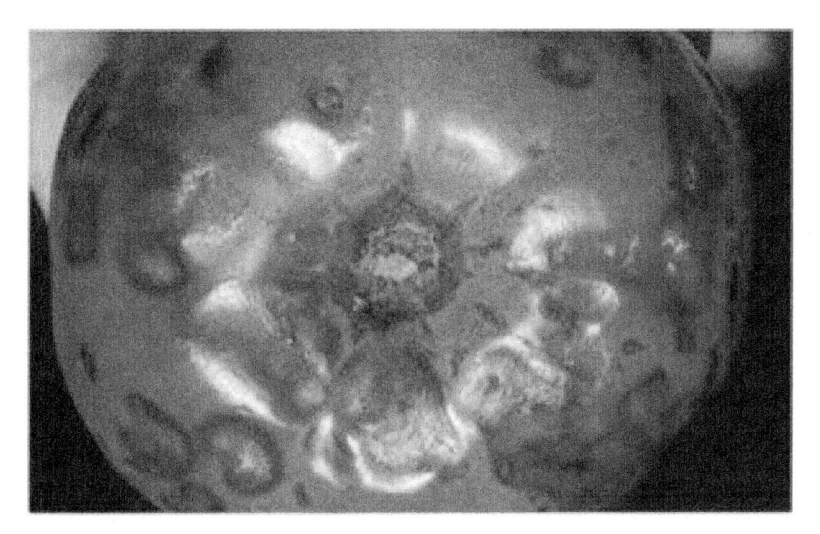

Cold damage in tomato

Hence the importance of worrying about factors such as using a nutrient solution appropriate to the crop's requirements, verifying pH and electrical conductivity, and keeping in mind the temperature requirements of the species to be cultivated.

Mushrooms

As already indicated, this group of microorganisms is the most important from the economic point of view in terms of their frequency of occurrence and the damage they can cause. In general, they can be classified based on the organs of the plant that affect, finding fungi associated with foliage (leaves and leaflets), others that affect the fruit, some that are located in the conductive vessels of the stem and finally those that attack the radical plant system.

In the same way, these phytopathogenic agents can produce quite different symptoms, such as necrotic spots on leaves, leaflets and stems, yellowing of foliage, loss of turgor, and wilting, internal necrosis on stems and roots, radical rot and fruit rot. Associated with this, in some cases, it is possible to observe the development of the fungus on the affected tissue, which can greatly facilitate the diagnosis.

These organisms usually reproduce through spores, which can be disseminated by water, wind, and even insects. These dissemination structures can be formed either through sexual or asexual mechanisms.

Bacteria

This group of pathogens is probably the second most important, after fungi; if we consider the number and severity of the diseases it produces. They can be considered as the smallest organisms capable of developing independently, unlike viruses. They are usually spherical or rod-shaped and can be found grouped in clusters, chains, or other forms (Goto, 1990). On the other hand, they can multiply rapidly through the process known as binary fission, being able to double their population in periods as short as 20 minutes.

Many diseases caused by bacteria can be determined with some degree of safety by the type of symptoms they produce in the plant. In addition, most are quite specific in terms of the host — for example, Pseudomonas syringae PV. Tomato, which causes bacterial freckle in tomato, produces small necrotic spots on the leaflets, always surrounded by a very characteristic chlorotic halo (Blancard, 1990).

Phytopathogenic bacteria can survive for prolonged periods in soil and plant debris as saprophytes, or in weeds as epiphytic populations. In this way, through splashing water, they can spread and start a new infection.

Some may even disperse through contaminated soil dragged by the wind, as demonstrated for Clavibacter michiganensis subsp. michiganensis, causative of bacterial canker of tomato, one of the main diseases in this crop. This bacterium, like others, can also easily move through contaminated tools, hands, or clothing, in this case, becoming important as a control measure of hygiene within our crop. Currently, about 60 species of bacteria causing disease in plants are recognized, including approximately 300 subspecies and pathovars. Among the most important pathologies caused by this type of pathogen, those that affect vegetables produced by bacteria of the genera Xanthomonas spp., Pseudomonas spp. And Clavibacter spp. Thus, we can mention an angular spot in Cucurbitaceae, bacterial spot, and bacterial freckle in tomato and bacterial canker of tomato (Blancard, 1990; Sherf and Macnab, 1986; Apablaza, 1999).

Viruses

Viruses are intracellular pathogens causing numerous losses in cultivated plants, being one of the main factors limiting production.

The losses caused by these phytopathogenic agents in extensive crops, fruit, and vegetables, are estimated at about 15 billion dollars annually worldwide (Hull, 2002).

In the absence of curative control measures for these types of diseases, the fight against these pathogens has been based on preventive measures such as cultural practices, which include control of vector agents, elimination of sources of infection, use of virus-free propagation material. And modification in the sowing or planting dates, among others.

The use of resistant cultivars developed through traditional breeding programs or obtained using parts of the pathogen genome in transgenic plants are also used (Baulcombe, 1996). Viruses, in general, have some quite characteristic symptoms; however, others can be confused with those caused by the action of abiotic agents such as the nutritional deficit, lack or excess of water, toxicity by chemical products (pesticides and herbicides), or soil problems (Jarvis, 2001b). For this reason, it is always suggestible to rule out other possible causes before attributing a particular symptom to a disease of a viral nature.

Among the most common symptoms caused by viruses, we can mention the color changes in leaves and fruits (mosaic and mottled) that correspond to areas of different colors (light green or usually yellow) alternated with the normal coloration of these structures. These color changes can also be manifested as chlorosis and banded veins in leaves and chlorotic or necrotic rings in leaves, stems, and fruits (Hull, 2002).

Leaf blisters caused by Watermelon Mosaic Virus (WMV) in melon

Other symptoms of this type of the disease are alterations in growth, such as shortening of internodes, changes in the morphology of some structures (deformation of fruits, leaf stabbing and blistering), uneven or out of time sprouting. A floral or fruit abortion can also occur, which will also ultimately affect performance.

Viruses, unlike other phytopathogenic organisms, are passively transmitted through different vector agents. Thus, among others, we can mention seeds, pollen, insects, mites, nematodes, and fungi. Similarly, vegetative structures (stakes, rhizomes, tubers) of propagation can also be an efficient way of disseminating viruses. Mechanical transmission through the sap can be another way through which some viruses can spread in the field, such as the Tobacco mosaic virus-TMV.

The transmission of viruses by insects, from an economic point of view, is the most important. Most virus vector insects have a sucking mouth device (aphids, scars-prawns, white mosquitoes, belonging to the Homopteran order), although some are also chewers (beetles) or have a scraping mouth apparatus (trips). Similarly, some mites (erythroid) have the ability to transmit viruses, although economically, they are much less important.

Virus diseases have been described for most of the plant species of economic importance. However, there are some diseases caused by these phytopathogenic agents, which are of greater importance in certain crops.

Myths and Mistakes to Avoid

Myths

Hydroponics Is A New Technology

This is a very common myth that is very popular amongst the traditionalists among us. However, as said earlier, it is just a myth. Hydroponic gardening is a very old and ancient field. It is believed that the pharaohs of Egypt loved fruits and vegetables that were grown hydroponically. Even the famous wonder of the Ancient World, The Hanging Gardens of Babylon, were supposed to be hydroponic gardens. In India, plants are grown directly in a coconut husk; hydro at the most grassroots level. It is thus proven that hydroponic gardening is not at all a new technique but an old and ancient science of cultivation.

Hydroponics Is Artificial Or Unnatural

Once again, this myth is highly popular amongst the traditional thinkers. Such people think that growing plants in water is against nature and is artificial. This is absolute rubbish. The growth of plants is a real and naturally occurring thing and cannot be done artificially. Plants need certain things to grow and thrive and they normally take these things from the soil. In hydroponics, we just replace the soil with water. Plants still can absorb whatever they need from the water and grow well. Unless you consider water unnatural, then you simply cannot consider hydroponic gardening unnatural.

Hydroponic gardening does not involve any kind of genetic mutation or introduction of any unwarranted and mysterious chemicals. This is not a steroid inducing system but is a perfectly natural and safe method of growing crops.

Hydroponics Harms The Environment

This is a ridiculous myth. Hydroponic gardening does not harm the environment at all. In fact, it helps the environment. Water is one of our most precious resources and because of hydroponic gardening around 70 to 90 % of water can be saved as compared to the conventional form of gardening. Hydroponic gardening also does not have any fertilizer runoff. This runoff can pollute the soil and rivers, lakes, etc.

Hydroponics is Very Complicated and Cannot Be Done at Home Unless You Are Exceptionally Talented

Hydroponics is a very easy system of gardening that can be done by almost anyone with a love of plants. An inexpensive hydroponic system can be constructed with simple things such as a bucket, hydroponic growing medium, and hydroponic nutrients. You can definitely use advanced technology and science to create an exceptionally sophisticated hydroponic garden to produce high amounts of yield, but you can also use simple, cheap, yet effective instruments and equipment if you want to do hydroponic gardening just as a hobby. As said earlier anyone can pick up hydroponic gardening, anyone means people of all ages.

Hydroponics Is Far Too Expensive

You can definitely use expensive and advanced technology and science to create an exceptionally sophisticated hydroponic garden to produce high amounts of yield, but you can also use simple, cheap, yet effective instruments and equipment if you want to do hydroponic gardening just as a hobby. You can work on a limited budget yet produce excellent and fantastic results with ease if you are dedicated to your garden.

Not Widespread And Limited To Developed Nations

This is a rather bizarre and ridiculous myth. Hydroponic gardening is done in every corner of the world.
People do hydroponic gardening in places where the climate is unsuitable for the growth of plants or in nations where the quality of soil is not suitable for a good yield. It is also commonly used in developed and developing nations such as the USA where the soil has been abused and is no longer cultivable. In British Columbia, 90% of all the greenhouse industry is now based upon the hydroponic gardening system.

Hydroponics Must Be Done Indoors

Hydroponics is generally cultivated indoors because people have no place to cultivate plants outside but relax. You can easily grow a hydroponic garden outdoors as well. A benefit of constructing a hydroponic garden indoors is the fact that you can control the lights. Outdoors you need to depend on the sun for the light. It not impossible or hard to do hydroponic gardening outdoors. It is even possible to do soil gardening inside the house if you know how to do it.

Hydroponics Don't Need Pesticides

Well this myth is very common but unfortunately false. You do need pesticides for a hydroponic garden, but the soil-born pests are eliminated naturally because of there being no soil. There are other kinds of pests that you need to protect your plants from. You should ideally only use pesticides when you feel that your plants are under attack. To avoid the attack of pests, keep a close eye on your system. Never enter the dark room when you are unclean or have come from outdoors especially from a garden or a park.

Hydroponics Produce Huge Plants

This myth is slightly true. Every seed like every other living thing has a genetic code that has all the coding that determines the size, weight, yield, etc. of the plant that the seed will produce. Hydroponics is a well-developed system, but it is not a magical system that can force a seed of cherry tomato to grow a beefsteak tomato plant. Yes, it can help you to grow the best cherry tomatoes with the seed though.

It is quite hard to grow a seed to its highest point in soil as the makeup of the soil varies from place to place. Although the components of the soil can be controlled and manipulated, you cannot have 100% control over them. However, in the case of hydroponic gardening you have total control and freedom on the components. You can easily manipulate them, so as to grow the best plants easily. Hydroponic gardening also consumes a lesser amount of energy as compared to soil gardening. This reserved energy is used by the plants to produce more and more yield. The plants become healthy, their foliage is dense and their flower and fruits delightful.

Hydroponics Is Used Primarily For Illegal Purposes

This myth, unfortunately, has some truth in it. However, like every other thing in this world, you can use hydroponics for a good purpose as well as a bad purpose. Sugar is a very tasty and sweet product but if used wrongly, it can give you diabetes. Similarly, dynamite is a very useful product but if used in an improper way, it can be dangerous. Hydroponic gardening is no different.

Often, law enforcement officials talk about hydroponic gardening when talking about marijuana and such illegal substances. Many people thus form a relationship or connection between two things and start believing that hydroponics is exclusively used to grow illegal substances.

Yes, it is true that people do use hydroponic systems for illegal purposes, but people use cars for illegal purposes too. If you cannot stop using cars, you should not stop using hydroponic gardening as an alternative kind of gardening. Remember, any power is good only until it is in safe hands. Power itself is not corrupt. The people who use it are corrupt. Likewise, hydroponic gardening is not wrong or illegal.

The corrupt people who use it for their illegal benefits are wrong.

Mistakes to Avoid

Since you are just now getting into hydroponics gardening, you may want to take things as slowly and as carefully as you could. One mistake could send the entire project rolling down the hill, and no one wants that. What an investment you have made, and how sad it would be to see it all amount to nothing! What you do to prevent this is to get first, a clear understanding of what your intended plants expect of you and how to attend to each of their needs.

While knowing what to do is important, you should also beware of what not to do, because doing so would mess up your project. Below is a review of common mistakes beginner hydroponic gardeners can make:

#1: Going Cheap by Sourcing Ineffective or Not Buying Enough Lighting

One of the most critical investments you ought to make as a hydroponic farmer is to seek the best lighting for your crops. This requires you to conduct first, substantial research in the market, and among seasoned hydroponic farmers, on the right kind of lighting, bearing in mind that different bulbs will produce different kinds of energy and light spectrums.

Also, don't expect that placing your plants next to a window is enough substitution for grow lights because usually, the light that gets in through the window is not sufficient, or strong enough to support the vigorous growth common among hydroponic plants.

#2: Designing Unusable or Difficult-To-Use Hydroponic Farms

Some beginners make the mistake of designing an unusable farm because they lack experience or because they have not dealt with hydroponics before, at least not on a large scale.

Due to inexperience, they fail to think about factors like efficiency and workflow, which leads to farms that make regular maintenance operations difficult, make harvesting difficult and do not use the space available efficiently. These inefficient gardens may also demand lots of tending, transplanting due to death of the plants, and difficulties controlling pests. Farmers also have a difficult time accessing various parts of the systems.

Now that labor is the most expensive variable cost in a farm, it is of great importance that the farms have labor-efficient designs.

The solution to this mistake is to take some considerable time to plan out and think about how the system will work, and from there, you can now build individual components. Consider all the variables, including water, nutrients, light, pests, convenience, access, redundancy, and automation, right from the start, and only start planning out the design once you have figured out each of the variables mentioned.

It would help if you went benchmarking, by visiting and talking to seasoned growers to see the systems they are operating. Go ahead and ask questions, including seeking answers to the question of what they would do differently were they to turn back and begin afresh.

#3: Confusing Biological Viability with Economic Viability

One of the misconceptions flying around the agricultural product markets is that establishing a farm requires 90% growing while selling takes 10%. However, when it comes to reality, the opposite is true, and many farmers make mistakes on either of the systems.

The farmers fail to take into consideration the financial costs and the time it would take for them to get their produce to the market once it has matured, and because of this small omission, many do not budget either money or the time that they would need to get their produce to the consumers. This effectively disrupts the schedule they had previously set for the farm and can lead to frustration due to lack of a market.

The second batch are those that go-ahead to plan for the biological functions of their farms, including the crops to grow, the techniques to use, and the equipment to source for, but they do all this without testing the feasibility of what they are producing in the market. They are not careful to ensure that what they are producing matches the local demand.

In the end, the farmers are frustrated at having a lot of produce and a facility, with no consumers to buy what they have grown.

The bottom line is that it will not matter how much effort you have dedicated to your farm, or how healthy and better tasting they are if no one wants them.

#4: Underestimating the Cost of Crop Production and Of Purchasing the Hydroponic System

It is typical of many motivated and determined hydroponic beginners to be so excited about getting into the hydroponic business that they underestimate just how they would have to spend to succeed at it. Beginners are often asked to start small and scale to bigger establishments with time, even if they feel like they have the resources they would need to go big. The problem is that some do not heed this instruction, and instead, they enter the industry and purchase large facilities, equipment, and expensive utilities.

Unfortunately, those who go ahead to start their gardens find that the costs of running hydroponic gardens are way too high, and some may quit in the middle of it due to the inadequacy of resources. Others do not even get to start the production process because by the time they finish purchasing the equipment and other resources, they no longer have any money to move ahead. The result is that in either case, the farmers do not get the chance to utilize their equipment fully due to unanticipated costs.

Therefore, as you make plans for your intended project, keep in mind costs like pest control, heat removal, replacement of equipment, labor, insurance, packaging, ongoing maintenance, and the cost of printing marketing materials. All these costs add up to a significant amount.

The most critical of the costs that are often underestimated is the cost of labor, whether the farmer is providing it himself or hiring someone to do it. If you are producing in rafts, for example, realize that it is a labor-intensive hydroponic production practice. The cost of labor for raft systems can go up to 45% or 60% of the total production costs. Many producers do not even take notice of this when calculating and making their estimates.

Therefore, when they get to the harvesting and processing stages, they are left in shock, not believing what their returns have become.

#5: Choosing the Wrong Market

The market for which you are producing is another critical factor that you ought to consider, whether your project is producing food to be sold later, or to be consumed by your family. If you grow crops that your market does not want, you will be wasting resources and opportunity. The result is that you will be trying to push your products on unwilling consumers, leading to wastage, and a loss of resources because you will not get a return on your investment.

Some crops are easy to grow, and when they are grown under hydroponics, their production is especially high. However, the crops are just unwanted. Therefore, before you decide on the crop you want to grow, conduct a proper analysis of your market, and even so, look at what your competition is growing. From there, come up with something that will give you lots of customers.

If you are living in an area where field producers present fierce competition with their produce, choose to produce what the producers cannot grow in that period. In most cases, if a consumer, say a restaurant, wants to buy organic lettuce and the field producer offers it at 50 cents a pound, the field producer will have the attention of the consumer, at least for the summer period, when he is producing.

When the seasonal competition is too stiff, come up with ways to survive and not lose your spot in the market. If you prove to be reliable, you will win the loyalty of many consumers, and you can lock them into permanent purchasing contracts, such that they will not even consider other producers, cheaper or not.

Conclusion

Indoor hydroponics has little effect on your growth during the season. Design your cultivation around the ease of your fresh foods requirements. We most want item in winter when high-quality vegetables are not in our local supermarket. Throughout my experience, I have found that salad and herbs are better grown in a different system from onions, tomatoes and peppers. The main reason that the herbs are grown separately is because they are very small in shape and would not grow well under vineyards when the light is close to the ceiling as the grape differs. Lettuce also yields higher in a very different combination of nutrients from vineyards. Finally, the lettuce is grown on a very short harvest period of 30 to 40 days, while the vines continue to grow up to six months or longer.

Lettuce can be sown every few days to supply approximately three transplants a week. It brings you salad to pick every day. The number of plants to cultivate depends on your individual demand for fresh salads. Herbs, with the exception of basil, initially grow very slowly. It takes about 3-4 months to develop well. You can harvest them every day, when they grow vigorously. For a full year, they will continue to grow.

Basil requires approximately 6 weeks to get well. The plants last up to 3 to 4 months if the basil is kept well tapped from the start. When the basil is 3 to 4 inches tall, pinch the tip of the wax or slice it after the second to third node with a scissor. This first cut allows plants to branch rather than if it is cut later and keeps the plants from becoming woody. Then cut the tops of every shoot by 3 inches back to the next or lower set of small shoots, which fork between the stick and leaves. Take this way to give you a plant with many branches that will have less woody growth. That's the trick with rising basil that I find. I personally have cultivated basil for up to six months or longer by regularly cutting it (harvesting). If it fails to bloom, it gets old or nervous. Pinch all the buds really early to keep them smaller. Sow typically approximately four plants per cube to create a plant bunch or cluster. These can be transplanted into the rising bed for 6 to 6 inches.

When you most want tomatoes, peppers, and cucumbers in winter, schedule the cultivation accordingly from November to March. Tomatoes will start to harvest fruit no later than mid-August until mid-November. A cropping cycle lasts 7 months until the end of March. Tomatoes need to be planted for about 100 days. Start a second crop by sowing seed at the beginning of March and start harvesting in June.

Greenhouse peppers take approximately one month longer to mature than tomatoes. It is best to start them in July and in March again. You can use bush varieties less mature than greenhouse varieties for a month or so. European cucumbers take 2 months from seeding to development of first fruit. If you want to grow all these crops in the same hydroponic system together, begin the cucumbers in September to prepare the cucumbers by November. Thus, the seedlings transplanted to your hydroponic system all start in the same size and grow together. It helps to raise the lights above all plants at the right level. It also prevents the shading of younger plants by older plants. You'll have two crops a year total. Start your seedlings in a separate system in your own sun, so that the current plant does not interfere with the transition.

Printed in Great Britain
by Amazon